Attitudes of a Transformed Heart

By
Martha Peace

Attitudes of a Transformed Heart
by Martha Peace

Scripture taken from the New American Standard Bible,
© 1960, 1962, 1963, 1971, 1972, 1973, 1975, 1977
by The Lockman Foundation.
Used by permission.

Cover design by Richard Schaefer

ISBN 1-885904-28-2

PRINTED IN THE UNITED STATES OF AMERICA
BY
FOCUS PUBLISHING INCORPORATED
Bemidji, Minnesota

Acknowledgements

The Lord has used many people to help with this book, but first and foremost is my husband, Sanford. Without his encouragement and help I would still be on chapter three! Another indispensable help was our daughter, Anna Maupin. Anna is my "English" person. She was the first one to read and edit the chapters and only once did she say of one particular section (which she made me take out), "Mom, this is boring!" Another vital editor was our pastor, John Crotts. Patiently he helped me understand the context of various Scriptures or reword explanations that were unclear. Toward the end of the process I would often say, "John, just please fix it!" And he would. My friend, Carol Young, took on the daunting task of checking each Scripture reference for accuracy. She did an excellent job and never once complained about how many there are! Our other two pastors, Kent Richards and Kent Keller, took time out of their very busy schedules to read the manuscript and give me many helpful comments. Only once did all three of our pastors react negatively to the same principle. So, I figured it must be God's Will for me to take that one out. Last, but certainly not least, are Jan Haley and Barb Smith from Focus Publishing. Jan and Barb edited my grammar, gave many good suggestions, and lovingly worked with me on several "difficult" sections. I also know that there are ladies who prayed for me during the process of writing this book and I thank God for each and every person who played a part.

Attitudes of a Transformed Heart has been a long time coming, and I am overwhelmed by the goodness and grace of the Lord Jesus Christ in my life to enable this project to come to a close. Suffice it to say, truly **He alone** is worthy!!

Martha Peace

*And do not be conformed to this world, but be
transformed by the renewing of your mind,
so that you may prove what the will of God is,
that which is good and acceptable and perfect.*
Romans 12:2

Table of Contents

Introduction

Part I - Attitudes about God

Part II - Attitudes and Scripture

Part III - Attitudes of Heart

Introduction

When I was a new baby Christian, I thought how amazing it is that God had made me completely holy. Actually, I felt holy. In that beginning time with the Lord, I marveled almost minute-by-minute about what the Lord Jesus Christ had done for me. His death on the cross for the payment of my sins astounded me and I loved thinking about it and how I was cleansed of my sin and forgiven. I was no longer in emotional agony as the wicked, who are *"like the tossing sea, for it cannot be quiet and its waters toss up refuse and mud"*(Isaiah 57:20). I was at peace because Christ's death ended my war with God. What a precious, wonderful time!

I am not sure how long my "cloud nine" experience lasted but I do remember the day when I found out, to my horror, that I still sinned. I knew that what I *did* could be a sin, but it was a real revelation when I read in Scripture that what I *thought* could also be a sin. I knew very little about Scripture but I knew one thing – I wanted to please the Lord more than anything else and if that meant I would have to change my thinking, then I would just have to change.

Since that beginning time as a Christian, I have learned more about how we grow and mature as Christians. As much as I wanted to believe myself instantaneously holy, I certainly was not. The process of making me holy had been begun by God and will be completed in heaven some day when I am with Him. Meanwhile, it will take a lifetime of God's grace enabling me to study the Scriptures and change my sinful thoughts and actions for me to become more and more like Christ. Prior to my salvation, I spent my life believing and embracing the views of the world. Often my view depended on what book or magazine I was reading or what school I was attending at the moment. All in all, I had been thoroughly brainwashed to believe the way others in the world believed. I did not know nor care what God's will was, much less that it was good and acceptable and perfect. I certainly needed to change.

As a Christian, however, I now had the God-given desire and capacity to change. As I read my Bible and heard good sermons, I was often confronted with wrong thinking on my part. Some examples of the right thoughts I had to adopt are: "God is good. He is always good! I am to obey Him whether I feel like it or not. Being overly sensitive and dwelling on hurt feelings is a manifestation of sinful pride. The feminist agenda is unbiblical. We are not to worship the earth. There are not multiple ways to God, only one. A person can say he is a Christian, yet not really be one. The Lord Jesus really will return but no one knows when. God's ways and thoughts are higher than ours. God is in charge whether we like it or not."

As my thoughts about God changed from the world's view to the Scriptural view, I saw Him more and more as lofty and exalted, high and lifted up. I saw Him not as a puppet to do my bidding but as my God Most High, much like Daniel's view of God. As I learned more and more of what the Bible taught about certain subjects, I began to apply what I learned to my life.

Since I became a Christian a little over twenty years ago, the Lord has changed me greatly. By that I mean my mind is being transformed and renewed. The more I learn what the Bible teaches about God and how we are to think and respond, the more like Christ I become. No, I am not holy as I thought I was as a new Christian (as a matter of fact, I still have a long way to go!), but I am by God's grace maturing into His character and way of thinking. My hope for this book is to share with you some of what I have learned over the past years. Even if you have been a committed Christian for many years, I would ask you to read this book prayerfully and ask God to show you any areas where you still may think as the world thinks. May God give you great grace and a teachable heart as you read the three parts of *Attitudes of a Transformed Heart* — Attitudes about God, Attitudes and Scripture, and Attitudes of Heart.

Part One

Attitudes About God

"I am the LORD, and there is no other;
Besides Me there is no God.
I will gird you, though you have not known Me;
That men may know from the rising to the setting of the sun
That there is no one besides Me;
I am the LORD, and there is no other."
Isaiah 45:5-6

Chapter 1

Daniel's View of God Most High

Some time ago, my husband, Sanford, and I had the opportunity to visit London, England, for the first time. I was struck by the prominence of the Queen. She was everywhere — her picture is on the money, her portrait in most buildings, and her initials on the front of the uniforms of the famous Beef Eaters. Previous kings and queens are also memorialized in conspicuous places. Queen Victoria's statue looms large in front of Buckingham Palace and the tombs of long dead monarchs are scattered throughout Westminster Abbey.

Here in America we would hardly think of bowing down to another person, but in England it is a ceremony they have embraced for centuries. In fact, it was not terribly long ago that they would not only bow down to their king but would also obey him.

As I thought about the concept of bowing before a king or queen, I wondered if it might have been easier for us who live in the United States to grasp the reality of God being King over us if we had been raised under the leadership of a king instead of a president. However, after I went to England, I realized that many there are just as deceived in their view of God as are most Americans.

God wants us to have a high and proper view of Him and to bow before Him in complete allegiance. It does not matter whether you have lived in a nation with a King; what matters is that God must give you a new heart and thus the capacity, as well as the desire, to bow before Him.

The cry of the New Testament church was "Jesus is Lord!" They rejected the idea that Caesar was their god and King. Those new believers saw the Lord Jesus Christ in the same way as Daniel saw *God Most High*. It seems that they had a right understanding of who God was and what He was like. They bowed before Him and worshiped Him, realizing that He was their High King.

To the extent that the new believers in Jerusalem did rightly understand Jesus as their Lord and King, their thoughts and beliefs about Him were right. To the extent, on the other hand, that their understanding was deficient, their thoughts and beliefs were conformed to the world's way of thinking. The same holds true today. There is no end to the ways sinful man can twist and pervert his understanding of what God is really like.

Man perverts his concept of God by inventing a god in his mind who is comfortable for him. For example, some believe God to be an enhanced version of Santa Claus. He sits in heaven and if you are good, He will give you the presents you deserve. Others take the view of a popular television talk show host. On one of his talk shows several years ago, he interviewed Christians. There was debate over who Jesus was. As I watched, the host explained his personal view of what God is like. His explanation went something like this, "Someday we'll all stand before God at the Judgment and He will be angry with us. He will point His finger at us and say, 'Why did you do ...?' Then suddenly He will change His mind and say, 'Oh, what the heck, come on in (to heaven) anyway.'"

Others may view God as angry, mean, hard, and poised to punish us at every turn. It is not difficult to find religious systems with pastors or leaders who control people with unbiblical threats and fear of what God is going to do next. Often these religions are outwardly full of beautiful rituals and religious splendor. They seem to have a high view of God, but in reality do not know God at all.

Then there is another view of God — a compassionate God who would never send anyone to hell. This god is basically a big wimp who is rather helpless to stop bad things from happening to good people. "After all," they would say, "God loves everybody and a loving God could never cause or permit bad things to happen to you. Therefore, He must be powerless to stop it."

Last, but certainly not least, is another spin on the "inflated view of man" concept of God. In this view man is ultimately captain of his own fate. He chooses God if and when he pleases. He can take God or leave Him. In this view, man is sovereign and God is not.

Many educated people do not believe there is a God, but those who do tend to have a tolerant and open-minded view of God. In other words, all God is concerned about is that we be sincere in whatever we believe and that we do our very best. These people are themselves tolerant of any and all (however bizarre) viewpoints of God. There is, however, one view they usually will not tolerate — the view that there is only one true way to think about God. The Lord Jesus clearly affirmed the view they reject when He said, **"No man comes unto the Father but through Me"** (John 14:6).

2

All of these except the Lord Jesus' view have something in common — they describe a god who does not exist! Instead of describing the God of the Bible, they are figments of man's very vivid imagination. The view that I clung to before I became a Christian was that it did not matter what you believed as long as you were sincere. I got this idea from the George Burns and John Denver movie, *Oh, God!* In that movie, George Burns (playing God) told John Denver, "Jesus is my son, Buddha is my son, and Mohammed is my son." In other words, it does not matter which way you choose to approach God. It made sense to me at the time.

In my mind God was like an enhanced version of the modern, educated, open-minded, tolerant American. I had a very low view of God and a very high view of myself. A high and holy view of God is one that sees Him and responds to Him as He is revealed in the Bible. It is a view that only God can give you and it changes your life forever.

When I think of someone who respected God and held a high and holy view of Him, I think of Daniel. As a new Christian, I remember reading about Daniel in the Old Testament. As I read I was moved by how Daniel talked about God, spoke of God to others, and prayed to God. He had a deep respect for God and for God's rule as King over himself as well as the entire world. God was very big in Daniel's mind and life and consequently men (even great and powerful kings) were comparatively very small. Not even the most powerful king in the world could intimidate Daniel because Daniel knew where the real power lay—in God's hands. Through Daniel's story we see that Daniel was much more concerned about promoting God's glory than he was in protecting himself.

The Story of Daniel and God Most High

In 605 B.C. Nebuchadnezzar was the King of Babylon. Babylon was the most powerful nation in the world. King Nebuchadnezzar had conquered Judah (the southern section of Israel) just as God had previously prophesied through Isaiah and Jeremiah. Nebuchadnezzar took captives from fallen Judah back to Babylon as slaves and prisoners. One of them was the young man Daniel.

Daniel was one of a group of four Jewish men who were chosen to serve the King and to give him wise advice. The other three, you will probably remember, are best known by their Babylonian names - Shadrach, Meschach, and Abednego.

Daniel ended up being in Babylon for seventy plus years. During that time, a great deal happened. Even though Nebuchadnezzar was his "larger than life" earthly king, Daniel tenaciously gave his ultimate allegiance to God. Often that allegiance was shown through Daniel's reaction to circumstances as well as in the names and titles that he gave to God. Let us consider some of those circumstances and names of God.

Taken to Serve in Nebuchadnezzar's Court

Then the king ordered Ashpenaz, the chief of his officials,
to bring in some of the sons of Israel, including some of
the royal family and of the nobles, youths in whom was
no defect, who were good-looking, showing intelligence
in every branch of wisdom, endowed with understanding
and discerning knowledge, and who had ability for serv-
ing in the king's court, and he ordered him to teach them
the literature and language of the Chaldeans.
Daniel 1:3-4

In addition to their education, the young men were to receive the king's choice food and wine to make them strong and healthy. However, this order created a dilemma for Daniel, Shadrach, Meschach, and Abednego. To comply with the king's orders meant they would have to defile themselves with the king's food and drink. If they did not comply, they risked death since Nebuchadnezzar had the power to kill at the slightest whim. In spite of the extreme risk, Daniel *"made up his mind that he would not defile himself with the king's choice food or with the wine..."* (Daniel 1:8, emphasis added). He decided to seek permission from the official in authority over him not to have to eat what the King decreed. God granted Daniel favor and the official agreed to allow Daniel, Shadrach, Meschach, and Abednego to choose their own food for a time. At the end of the allotted time, Daniel and the others were so much healthier that the official granted them permission to continue to eat as God had commanded. Daniel saw God and God's Law as that of a King higher than Nebuchadnezzar.

Time went on, however, and ...

The King had a Dream

Nebuchadnezzar was troubled by his dream. He sought counsel from his wise men as to the meaning of the dream. He ordered them not only to tell him the meaning of the dream but also to tell him what the dream was in the first place. Obviously this was going to be impossible for mere men. So the Babylonian wise men appealed to the King. Merciless, Nebuchadnezzar was adamant.

The command from me is firm: if you do not make known to me the dream and its interpretation, you will be torn limb from limb and your houses will be made a rubbish heap. But if you declare the dream and its interpretation, you will receive from me gifts and a reward and great honor; therefore declare to me the dream and its interpretation.   Daniel 2:5-6

What a mess these men found themselves in all because the King got up on the wrong side of the bed! They could not tell him his dream and so the order went out to kill them all. Unfortunately, that included Daniel.

Daniel turned to God for help. He requested compassion from the *God of heaven*. God granted Daniel knowledge of the dream and the interpretation. Daniel was exceedingly grateful. Listen to how Daniel thanked his high and holy God.

Let the name of God be blessed forever and ever, for wisdom and power belong to Him. It is He who changes the times and the epochs; He removes kings and establishes kings; He gives wisdom to wise men. And knowledge to men of understanding. It is He who reveals the profound and hidden things; He knows what is in the darkness and the light dwells with Him. To You, <u>O God of my fathers</u>, I give thanks and praise, for You have given me wisdom and power; even now You have made known to me what we requested of You, for You have made known to us the king's matter.   Daniel 2:20-23 (emphasis added)

Daniel gave thanks and credit to God whom he called the *God of my fathers.* Daniel clearly gave God all the credit for Daniel's wisdom and understanding as he explained to Nebuchadnezzar the dream and its interpretation. The dream was about a strange statue that was made of different metals and compounds — gold, silver, bronze, clay and iron. Each part of the statue represented an earthly kingdom that would eventually end, but God's kingdom would endure forever.

Daniel Explains the Dream to King Nebuchadnezzar

In the days of those kings the <u>God of heaven</u> will set up a kingdom which will never be destroyed, and that king-

> *dom will not be left for another people; it will crush and put an end to all these kingdoms, but it will itself endure forever. Inasmuch as you saw that a stone was cut out of the mountain without hands and that it crushed the iron, the bronze, the clay, the silver and the gold, <u>the great God</u> has made known to the king what will take place in the future; so the dream is true and its interpretation is trustworthy.*   *Daniel 2:44-45, emphasis added*

King Nebuchadnezzar realized that only the true God could have given Daniel the dream and its interpretation. He answered Daniel ...

> *Surely your God is a <u>God of gods</u> and a <u>Lord of kings</u> and a revealer of mysteries, since you have been able to reveal this mystery.*   *Daniel 2:47, emphasis added*

You would think that Nebuchadnezzar would bow before and begin to worship Daniel's "great God" whom Nebuchadnezzar himself called the "God of gods" and the "Lord of kings." However, he did just the opposite. He built a ninety foot tall gold statue of himself so that everyone else could worship him!

Of course, neither Daniel, nor his friends (Shadrach, Meschach, and Abednego) would bow down and worship King Nebuchadnezzar. Some jealous Babylonians took advantage of this opportunity and reported to the King that neither Shadrach, Meshach, nor Abednego, were obeying the King's order to worship him. Nebuchadnezzar was furious and ordered the three of them bound by ropes and cast into the furnace of blazing fire. Before they were thrown into the furnace, he gave them one last chance, but:

> *Shadrach, Meshach and Abednego replied to the king, "O Nebuchadnezzar, we do not need to give you an answer concerning this. If it be so, <u>our God</u> whom we serve is able to deliver us from the furnace of blazing fire; and He will deliver us out of your hand, O king. But even if He does not, let it be known to you, O king, that we are not going to serve your gods or worship the golden image that you have set up."*   *Daniel 3:16-18, emphasis added*

Their faith in God was unshakable in spite of the extreme danger. Perhaps you remember the rest of the story. Those tending to the fire (including the King) watched the gruesome process and were astounded as they saw not three men, but four, (apparently the Lord Jesus Christ was with them) walking around un-scathed and unbound in the fire. Their *great God* did deliver them and when they stepped out of the blazing furnace, their hair and clothes did not even smell of smoke.

King Nebuchadnezzar was so astonished that he made a new decree that if anyone spoke anything offensive against the God of Shadrach, Meshach, and Abednego, they were to be killed. Actually as Nebuchadnezzar so poetically put things, they were to be **"torn limb from limb and their houses made a rubbish heap!"** (Daniel 3:29).

Time went on and Nebuchadnezzar had another disturbing dream. It was a strange dream about a large, fruitful tree that was chopped down by some sort of angel. A resulting stump was left and the angel announced **"And let him share with the beasts in the grass ... and let a beast's mind be given to him"** (Daniel 4:15-16). The angel's point being —

> *In order that the living may know that the <u>Most High</u> is*
> *ruler over the realm of mankind and bestows it on whom*
> *He wishes and sets over it the lowliest of men.*
> *Daniel 4:17, emphasis added*

Not surprisingly, Daniel was the only one who could interpret the dream. This time, even Daniel was frightened. He was **"appalled for a while as his thoughts alarmed him"** (Daniel 4:19). The King assured Daniel that it was per-missible to tell the interpretation.

Daniel Explains the Second Dream

> *The tree that you saw...is you, O king; for you have*
> *become great and grown strong, and your majesty has*
> *become great and reached to the sky and your dominion*
> *to the end of the earth. ...This is the interpretation (of the*
> *rest of the dream). This is the decree of the <u>Most High</u>,*
> *which has come upon my lord the king: that you be driven*
> *away from mankind and your dwelling place be with the*
> *beasts of the field, and you be given grass to eat like cattle*
> *and be drenched with the dew of heaven; and seven peri-*
> *ods of time will pass over you, until you recognize that*
> *the <u>Most High</u> is ruler over the realm of mankind and*
> *bestows it on whomever He wishes...your kingdom will*

> *be assured to you after you recognize that it is <u>Heaven</u>
> that rules. Therefore, O king, may my advice be pleasing
> to you: break away now from your sins by doing righ-
> teousness and from your iniquities by showing mercy to
> the poor, in case there may be a prolonging of your pros-
> perity."*   *Daniel 4:20-27, emphasis added*

Even though Daniel was greatly afraid to tell Nebuchadnezzar, Daniel gave the interpretation stating that Nebuchadnezzar must bow before Daniel's God who is Most High and truly rules. Unfortunately for King Nebuchadnezzar, he did not heed Daniel's advice. Consequently, God temporarily removed sovereignty from the King and Nebuchadnezzar became a madman, living in the wild and eating grass like an animal. Eventually, Nebuchadnezzar's reason returned. This is what happened.

> *But at the end of that period, I, Nebuchadnezzar, raised
> my eyes toward heaven and my reason returned to me,
> and I blessed the <u>Most High</u> and praised and honored Him
> who lives forever; For His dominion is an everlasting
> dominion, and His kingdom endures from generation to
> generation. All the inhabitants of the earth are accounted
> as nothing, but He does according to His will in the host
> of heaven and no one can ward off His hand or say to
> Him, "What have you done?" At that time my reason re-
> turned to me. And my majesty and splendor were restored
> to me for the glory of my kingdom, and my counselors
> and my nobles began seeking me out; so I was reestab-
> lished in my sovereignty, and surpassing greatness was
> added to me. Now, I, Nebuchadnezzar, praise, exalt and
> honor the <u>King of Heaven,</u> for all His works are true and
> His ways just, and He is able to humble those who walk
> in pride.*
>   *Daniel 4:34-37, emphasis added*

Now, not only Daniel, but also Nebuchadnezzar held to a high and proper view of God.

Conclusion

Daniel's consuming passion was God — *the* God Most High, King of heaven. He lived his life in Babylon rightly respecting and revering God. He never forgot the God of his fathers. Daniel often faced death because he consistently chose to follow God, and in the process, God used Daniel mightily to proclaim His glory. Daniel's God was *great*. Instead of seeking to have his own needs met, Daniel saw himself there to serve God on God's terms, no matter the cost.

What about you? Who are you worshiping and serving — yourself or Daniel's great God? Do you have a high and proper (truly Scriptural) view of God or do you believe He is merely your puppet existing to make you feel worthy and special? Earthly monarchs come and go but there is only one high King — the One who is King over all the kings — God Most High.

Before we learn more about God Most High and His relationship with man in the next chapters, take a few moments to pray and ask God to help you bow before Him, serve Him and honor Him by thinking thoughts about Him that are not conformed to the world's way of thinking. It may mean some of your previous beliefs about man and God must change. If so, what is your prayer?

∞

Chapter 1

Study Questions

1. How might man pervert his concept of God?
   Give three examples.

2. Instead of a variety of ways, what did the Lord Jesus say about how we come to God? See John 14:6.

3. As you answer the questions in this chapter, make a list of the names of God that you come across.

4. What was more important to Daniel than his own personal safety?

5. How did Daniel get from Judah to Babylon?

6. What was Daniel's assignment after he got to Babylon?

7. According to Daniel chapter one, what was the first test that Daniel faced?

8. When King Nebuchadnezzar threatened to kill the wise men (including Daniel) if they could not interpret his dream, to whom did Daniel turn for help?

9. What do you learn about God from Daniel 2:20-23?

10. According to the last paragraph on page 5 and according to Daniel 2:44-45, what is the difference between the kingdom the statue represented and God's kingdom?

11. After Daniel gave the interpretation of the first dream, what did King Nebuchadnezzar do?

12. How did Shadrach, Meshack, and Abednego end up in the fiery furnace? What was their attitude right before they were thrown into the furnace?

13. Why was Daniel afraid to tell King Nebuchadnezzar the interpretation of the second dream?

14. What were the consequences for King Nebuchadnezzar when he did not heed Daniel's advice? See Daniel 4:20-27.

15. According to the first paragraph in the conclusion of this chapter, how did Daniel view God?

Chapter 2

Religious Man "Most High"

As we learned from the previous chapter, Daniel viewed God as high and exalted. He often called Him "God Most High". He prayed to the "God of Heaven". He had great respect and reverence for God. On more than one occasion, he risked his life rather than dishonor God. Daniel had a right view of God and of himself. He was religious in a good sense (James 1:27). Instead of being enamored with his own ability to impress God, He loved God and was faithfully devoted to Him. Daniel was not like many Christians today who have unbiblical views of God and man. Rather than seeing God as "Most High," they see <u>man</u> as "Most High" while God is somewhere in the background. A wrong view of God, logically, will result in a wrong view of man. In order that we will not hold to a wrong view of man or God, I want to explain who "Man Most High" is and what is wrong with thinking of man in this way.

Man Most High

"Man Most High" is an unbiblical view of mankind that is man-centered and man-esteeming instead of God-centered and God-esteeming. Of course all men have God-given value in that they are created in God's image, but in the "Man Most High" view of man, man takes his quest for personal worth or goodness too far. In this view, man **"thinks more highly of himself than he ought to think"** (Romans 12:3). He seeks to find worth and glory for himself beyond what the Scripture allows. Instead, man should be seeking to call attention to the worth and glory of God. Although this view of man may seem to be merely two different ways to say the same thing, it results, nonetheless, in a false gospel and a wrong view of how Christians grow.

I tend to think of "Man Most High" in two broad categories: "Religious Man" and "Psychologized Man." Often he is a mixture of both. Regardless of which category one falls into "Man Most High" has been influenced by the world's wisdom and logic. Since God's ways and thoughts are higher than ours, what may seem perfectly logical to us may, in actuality, deceive us. The Apostle Paul sums up man's wisdom in 1 Corinthians 3:19-20:

> *For the wisdom of this world is foolishness before God. For it is written, "He is the one who catches the wise in their craftiness"; and again, "The LORD knows <u>the reasonings of the wise</u>, that they are useless."*
>
> *(emphasis added)*

The world's craftiness and reasonings are not only useless, but also potentially deadly as **"There is a way which seems right to a man, but its end is the way of death"** (Proverbs 14:12).

Since these issues are critical in order for one to have a high and proper view of God and to have a right understanding of man, this chapter is about "Religious Man Most High" and the next chapter is about "Psychologized Man Most High." Both have unbiblical beliefs about God that are often dependent upon man's logic and reasoning. This chapter explains some of the characteristics of religious man as well as how we should rightly think about man.

Religious Man

Religious man simply gives himself too much credit. He may believe that doing good works will earn him his salvation. You might hear someone say of religious man, "If anyone deserves to go to heaven it is that person. Look at all he has done."

The Bible makes it clear that no one deserves to go to heaven. In fact, if we got what we deserved it would be death and eternal punishment in hell. The Apostle Paul expressed it this way **"...by the works of the Law [doing good deeds] no flesh will be justified [declared righteous by God] in His [God's] sight..."** (Romans 3:20, explanation added). He also wrote in Romans 6:23 **"For the wages of sin is death, but the free gift of God is eternal life in Christ Jesus our Lord."** Because God is holy and we sin, we could never work hard enough or be good enough to go to heaven.

In addition to performing good works, sometimes religious man believes that taking the sacraments at church and being faithful to go to church will either save him or at least permit him to keep his salvation. This thought might be true if what we did could cause us to be saved in the first place, but it does not.

The children of Israel were certainly religious. They burned incense, offered sacrifices, and followed to the letter all of the feasts and religious festivals that God commanded them through Moses. You may be thinking, "So, what's wrong with that?" The problem was not that they *observed* the external rituals but what they *thought* about those rituals. They believed that the rituals made them acceptable to God. Consider what God told the Israelites through the Prophet Isaiah:

> *"What are your multiplied sacrifices to Me?" says the LORD. I have had enough of burnt offerings of rams and the fat of fed cattle; and I take no pleasure in the blood of bulls, lambs or goats. When you come to appear before Me, who requires of you this trampling of My courts? Bring your worthless offerings no longer, incense is an abomination to Me. New moon and Sabbath, the calling of assemblies - I cannot endure iniquity and the solemn assembly. I hate your new moon festivals and your appointed feasts, they have become a burden to Me; I am weary of bearing them. So when you spread out your hands in prayer, I will hide My eyes from you; Yes, even though you multiply prayers, I will not listen. Your hands are full of bloodshed."*   **Isaiah 1:11-15**

The Israelites problem was not that they were performing the ceremonies incorrectly, but the problem was that they came to offer sacrifices without a repentant attitude. Man (apart from God) is naturally religious and gives himself the benefit of the doubt as to his ability to please God and be acceptable to God.

In addition to thinking he can earn his salvation or at least keep it by performing good works, religious man never understands how utterly **"dead"** he really is in his **"trespasses and sins"** (Ephesians 2:1). By that I mean he may think that he is good enough that he can choose to be saved. You hear this proclaimed through Christian cliches such as, "Come forward and make a decision for Christ." A statement like this is based on the belief that man is free to decide for or against Christ. While it is true that man is responsible to repent and believe and that the offer of salvation is available to him, his will has been totally corrupted by sin. So marred, in fact, that he is blinded to his complete and utter dependence upon God to save him in the first place. Certainly God has a love for all mankind, but those who are called out of darkness into His marvelous light are drawn by God and given a desire by God to turn from their

15

sin and to give God glory. God is the one who chooses and saves and His choice is based on no goodness (or decision) within man. Left to himself, man would never choose God.

> *...for we have already charged that both Jews and Greeks are all under sin; as it is written, "There is none righteous, not even one; there is none who understands, <u>there is none who seeks for God</u>..."* Romans 3:9-10, emphasis added

> *Blessed be the God and Father of our Lord Jesus Christ, who has blessed us with every spiritual blessing in the heavenly places in Christ, <u>just as He chose us in Him</u> before the foundation of the world, that we would be holy and blameless before Him.* Ephesians 1:3-4, emphasis added

> *Jesus said, "No man can come unto Me unless <u>the Father</u> who sent Me <u>draws him</u>."* John 6:44, emphasis added

> *But you are a <u>chosen race,</u> a royal priesthood, a holy nation, a people for God's own possession, so that you may proclaim the excellencies of <u>Him who has called you</u> out of darkness into His marvelous light; for you once were not a people, but now you are the people of God; you had not received mercy but now you have received mercy.*
> 1 Peter 2:9-10, emphasis added

Religious man is deceived. He elevates himself and dethrones God. Because of his high view of himself (good enough to choose God or deserve His favor), he has a low view of God. His view is wrong. So, what then is ...

The Proper Perspective of Man

A.W. Tozer had a right perspective of man. He wrote of man's obligation to God.

> Man has a crushing burden — his obligation to God. It includes an instant and lifelong duty to love God with every power of mind and soul, to obey Him perfectly, and to worship Him acceptably. The gospel can lift this destroying burden from the mind, give beauty for ashes, and the garment of praise for the Spirit of heaviness. But unless the weight of the burden is felt the gospel can mean nothing to the man; and until he sees a vision of God high and lifted up, there will be no woe and no

burden. Low views of God destroy the gospel for all who hold them.[1]

Man's obligation to God cannot be realized through faithfully attending church, partaking of the sacraments, doing good works, or making a decision for Christ. Instead, to find answers in his search for God he must go to the only authoritative, completely truthful book that we have - the Bible. It is the Word of God which is **"living and active"** (Hebrews 4:12) from which we should formulate our beliefs, not from a deceitful heart. Think about the following biblical principles regarding man:

1. Man is made by God in His image.

    God created man in His own image, in the image of God He created him; male and female He created them.
    Genesis 1:27

2. Man is dead in his trespasses and sins apart from Christ.

    And you were dead in your trespasses and sins, in which you formerly walked according to the course of this world, according to the prince of the power of the air, of the spirit that is now working in the sons of disobedience. Among them we too all formerly lived in the lusts of our flesh, indulging the desires of the flesh and of the mind, and were by nature children of wrath, even as the rest.
    Ephesians 2:1-3

3. Man thinks more highly of himself than he ought.

    For through the grace given to me I say to every man among you not to think more highly of himself than he ought to think; but to think so as to have sound judgment, as God has allotted to each a measure of faith.
    Romans 12:3

    Do nothing from selfishness or empty conceit, but with humility of mind let each one of you regard one another as more important than yourselves; do not merely look out for your own personal interests, but also for the interest of others.
    Philippians 2:3-4

4. Man loves himself whether he is thinking how wonderful he is or he

is putting himself down in the grip of self-pity. Either way, his focus is sinfully on self.

> *But realize this, that in the last days difficult times will come. For men will be <u>lovers of self</u>... conceited...holding to a form of godliness, although they have denied its power..."*   *2 Timothy 3:1-5, emphasis added*

> *One of them, a lawyer, asked Him a question, testing Him, "Teacher, which is the great commandment in the Law? And He said to him, "You shall love the LORD your God with all your heart, and with all your soul, and with all your mind. This is the great and foremost commandment. The second is like it, You shall love your <u>neighbor as your-self</u>."*   *Matthew 22:35-39, emphasis added*

(Note - the Lord Jesus is not teaching here that we must love ourselves before we can love others. He is teaching the complete opposite, that if we loved others as much as we already love ourselves, we would be fulfilling the second great commandment.)

5. Man is enticed to sin by his own lusts.

> *Let no one say when he is tempted, "I am being tempted by God;" for God cannot be tempted by evil and He Himself does not tempt anyone. But each one is tempted when he is carried away and enticed by his own lust [desires or longings]. Then when lust has conceived, it gives birth to sin; and when sin is accomplished, it brings forth death. Do not be deceived, my beloved brethren."*
> *James 1:13-16, explanation added*

6. Man is responsible to God to repent and believe and therefore is in desperate need of Christ. Unless God draws him, convicts him of his sin, and grants him repentance, he will not believe God (in a "saving" sense), however religious he becomes.

> *Therefore having overlooked the times of ignorance, God is now declaring to men that all people everywhere should repent, because He has fixed a day in which He will judge the world in righteousness through a Man whom He has appointed, having furnished proof to all men by raising Him from the dead.*   *Acts 17:30-31*

...if you confess with your mouth Jesus as Lord, and believe in your heart that God raised Him from the dead, you will be saved; for with the heart a man believes, resulting in righteousness, and with the mouth he confesses resulting in salvation.   **Romans 10:9-10**

For by grace you have been saved through faith; and that not of yourselves, it is the gift of God; not as a result of works, so that no one may boast.   **Ephesians 2:8-9**

For we were once foolish ourselves, disobedient, deceived, enslaved to various lusts and pleasures, spending our life in malice and envy, hateful, hating one another. But when the kindness of God our Savior and His love for mankind appeared, He saved us, not on the basis of deeds which we have done in righteousness, but according to His mercy, by the washing of regeneration and renewing by the Holy Spirit, whom He poured out upon us richly through Jesus Christ our Savior, that being justified by His grace we might be made heirs according to the hope of eternal life.   **Titus 3:3-7**

Man is hopelessly lost without the Lord Jesus Christ. He does not have the capacity to turn in faith to Christ. God must draw him and give him the faith to trust the Lord Jesus exclusively for salvation and forgiveness of sins. If man were left to his own devices, he would never choose God. Instead, he would naturally give himself the benefit of the doubt when it comes to his ability to be good and thus earn, deserve, or choose God's favor. Apart from Christ, man is already spiritually dead in his sin and if he is not saved by God, he will someday not only be physically dead, but also eternally separated from God (See Isaiah 59:2 and Revelation 20:11-15). Only God has the power to make a person right with Him. Man is not "Most High," — God is. Man is completely dependent on his Creator.

Man is a created being, a derived and contingent self, who of himself possesses nothing but is dependent each moment for his existence upon the One who created him after His own likeness. That God is everything and man nothing is a basic tenet of Christian faith and devotion...Man for all his genius is but an echo of the original Voice, a reflection of the uncreated Light.[2]

Now that we have considered who religious man is and what is in his heart (how he thinks, feels, and decides), we need to bring these issues into our everyday thinking. In order to make certain that you have not been influenced to think about yourself in an unbiblically religious way, take a few minutes and carefully compare the differences in the following chart between "Right Ways to Think" as opposed to "Wrong Ways to Think." Pray that God will make you discerning about these issues.

WRONG WAYS TO THINK	RIGHT WAYS TO THINK
God loves me because I am so special and valuable.	God chose to love me and have mercy on me for His glory. Mercy is pity upon the pitiful. Praise God!
After all that I have done for the Lord, if anyone deserves to go to heaven it is me.	If I got what I deserved, it would be eternal punishment in hell.
I know that I am a Christian because I was born in a Christian family and have always gone to church.	No one is physically born a Christian. To become a Christian they have to be supernaturally reborn by the Spirit of God.
I know that I've been carnal for a long time but I must be a Christian because I prayed a prayer in church with the pastor when I was twelve years old.	Just because I prayed a prayer does not make me a Christian. If I were a Christian, I would have a love for the Lord Jesus and a desire to please Him. There would be genuine fruit in my life.
God, thank you that I am not like all those other sinners.	God, be merciful to me, the sinner. (see Luke 18:13)

Conclusion

Religious man is proud of himself. He believes that his good works or inherent goodness will save him or, at the very least, enable him to keep his salvation. He is deceived about the gospel, his sin, and his desperate need for Christ. His unbiblical logic tells him, "Join the church, be baptized, and do good works. If your good works outweigh your bad works, you will be saved." It also tells him, "Do you want to have a wonderful life and go to heaven when you die? Then simply make a decision for Christ by praying a certain prayer."

Man is (to use a Southern expression) "a mess!" We are proud, lovers of ourselves, and more sinful than we can even imagine. If you do not believe that you are sinful, think about the price your sin cost God - the very life of His beloved Son.

> *...knowing that you were not redeemed with perishable things like silver or gold from your futile way of life inherited from your forefather, but with precious blood, as of a lamb unblemished and spotless, the blood of Christ.*
> **1 Peter 1:18-19**

The only way we can be right with God is by His grace and mercy to us since it is not within religious man's ability to earn God's favor. The focus must be on what God has done, not on what we think we deserve. We are here to serve and glorify God, not ourselves.

In the next chapter, we'll see how psychologized man thinks and how his wrong thinking also needs to be **"transformed by the renewing of his mind"** (Romans 12:2).

Chapter 2

Study Questions

1. How has "Man Most High" been influenced?
   See the third paragraph in chapter two.

2. What is wrong with this statement - "Good people deserve
   to go to heaven."? See Romans 3:20 and Romans 6:23.

3. What was wrong with the religion of the children of Israel?
   See page 15.

4. Match the following statement with the Scripture:

"...There is none who seek for God..."	John 6:44
"...just as He chose us in Him before the foundation of the world..."	Romans 3:9-10
God the Father draws those who come to Christ.	1 Peter 2:9-10
It is God who calls Christians out of darkness into light.	Ephesians 1:3-4

5. List some of the ways that man cannot make himself right with God.

6. Where is the only place to find true answers concerning how we should view man?

7. True or False. Use Scripture to back up your answer:
   a. Man evolved from animals.

   b. Man is basically good.

   c. Man has an accurate view of himself.

   d. Man loves himself even when he is despairing in the grip of self-pity. That is because his focus is on himself.

   e. It is man's own longings or desires that cause him to be tempted to sin.

f. The more religious man is the more God is likely to save him.

8. See how many of the following wrong ways to think you
    can correct without looking at the chart on page 21.
    Afterwards go back and refer to the chart if you need to.
    a. God loves me because I am so special and valuable.

    b. After all that I have done for the Lord, if anyone deserves
        to go to heaven it is me.

    c. I know that I am a Christian because I was born in a
        Christian family and have always gone to church.

    d. I know that I've been carnal for a long time but I must be
        a Christian because I prayed a prayer in church with the
        pastor when I was twelve years old.

    e. God, thank you that I am not like all those other sinners.

9. According to 1 Peter 1:18-19, what are we not redeemed by and what are we redeemed by?

10. Refer to the next to the last paragraph in this chapter and fill in the following blanks: The only way we can be right with God is by His _____ and _____ to us. The focus must be on what God has done, not on what we think we _____.

11. To make sure that you are not like "Religious Man," complete the Bible study in the back of this book entitled "Salvation Work Sheets."

Chapter 3

Psychologized Man
"Most High"

One day I was working around the house and the radio was playing. A world-respected Christian psychologist was explaining how awful it is when one spouse calls the other spouse ugly names or puts them down. I agreed. At one point in his radio program, he asked, "Why is it wrong to call your spouse ugly names?" I stopped what I was doing and listened very carefully. I wanted to make certain that I understood his answer. He said, "Because it will tear down their self-esteem."

While I agree that name-calling is awful, I was grieved over his man-centered answer. He did not mention one word about God, His holiness, or about His being offended. Nor did he explain about sin and the devastating effects it has in marriage. Also nothing was said about the offended spouse's opportunity to glorify God (Matthew 5:16; 1 Corinthians 10:31), to overcome evil with good (Romans 12:21), to turn the other cheek (Matthew 5:39), to go the second mile (Matthew 5:41), to give a blessing instead (1 Peter 3:9), or to forgive (Ephesians 4:32). Unfortunately just as many of our psychologists have made "man" the focus of life, so have many of our churches.

Occasionally we receive advertisements in the mail from churches in our area. One that came last summer told volumes about that church's view of God. It contained blurbs like:

> "I go to _____Church because the skits they have on Sunday mornings help *my sense of belonging*."

> "I personally know what it is like to *feel like you don't belong*. Our church is committed to reach out and use whatever is necessary in order to say to the community that God cares about them.

We recognize the need for God and that people matter to Him and we are trying to be the church for the rest of us who haven't yet experienced this truth."

These advertisements are subtly focused on man and his needs rather than God. They are a far cry from hearing, "Come to our church to glorify God. We preach detailed sermons based on Scripture. We strive to leave with a deeper understanding of God, His holiness, His love, and our sin. We must repent of our sin. We are here to serve, exalt, and glorify God through having a high and proper view of Him."

If our mind is to be transformed to think Scriptural beliefs about God, we must also have a biblically accurate view of man. In order to have this biblically accurate opinion of man, it is crucial that we formulate our view from the Scriptures (such as Genesis 1:26-27; Ephesians 2:1). We must be especially careful not to base our thoughts about man on psychological theory, some church flyers, many ladies' seminars, or the bulk of what is currently popular in Christian bookstores and on Christian radio. Because society (even the Christian society) today is being bombarded with "Man" instead of God, I thought it appropriate to study "Psychologized Man Most High."

Psychologized Man

To best explain psychologized man, we need to begin with an example. Suppose Sue, a woman in her thirties, is experiencing anxiety or depression. Viewing her through a psychology lens, her counselor would probably want to help her get in touch with her deep emotional pain. She may not even know what is causing her depression or anxiety, but it is assumed by her counselor to be somehow coming from repressed trauma (hurts, rejection, etc.) within the subconscious part of herself.

To locate the cause of her emotional pain, Sue must go back into her past, uncover those "supposed" unconscious or subconscious drives and re-experience the pain inflicted on her by others (often her parents). Unfortunately, she may have to suffer greatly in the process. Only after she has experienced the deepest level of this emotional pain (through countless hours of talking about her feelings, hypnotherapy, pages of journaling, and/or participation in group therapy) can she then (in a Christianized version of this psychological process) turn to Christ and begin to heal. Her Christian therapist may conclude that her anxiety or depression was caused by feelings of worthlessness from not having her need for love or security met when she was a child. Her emotional pain is viewed as having been fed by unconscious thoughts that were somehow stirring up her negative emotions or fear. If she could, through her therapy, experience her deepest pain and come to understand who she is *in Christ*, then she could experience emotional healing.

In order to understand what is faulty in this line of reasoning, we need to explain Sigmund Freud's concept of the unconscious. As well, we need to think through Abraham Maslow's "Hierarchy of Needs" and Erik Erikson's teaching on "identity crisis." Let's begin with Freud.

Sigmund Freud's Concept of the Unconscious

Sigmund Freud, the founder of psychoanalysis, lived from 1856-1939. He was an Austrian physician who has greatly influenced the world's way of thinking about how to help people with their problems. His work progressed through stages that began with a book explaining how the "symptoms of hysteria were ascribed to manifestations of undischarged emotional energy associated with forgotten psychic traumas."[3] Freud, and co-author, Josef Breuer, believed the way to help people prone to hysteria was to uncover their repressed traumas through hypnosis.

In a hypnotic state the patient would be led by the therapist to recall and reenact the traumatic experience. Thus he would be purged of the hysteria-producing emotions. Soon, however, Freud abandoned hypnosis and substituted what he termed "free association." Using free association, the therapist investigates "spontaneous flow of thoughts to reveal the unconscious mental processes at the root of the neurotic disturbance."[4] So, through hours of talking about whatever comes to mind, the patient reveals (and the doctor would interpret) his unconscious drives.

Next came Freud's teaching on repression and resistance. Repression, Freud believed, is a "device operating unconsciously to make the memory of painful or threatening events inaccessible to the conscious mind."[5] Resistance, on the other hand, is an "unconscious defense against awareness of repressed experiences in order to avoid the resulting anxiety."[6] Freud believed that there were two basic forces of the mind – the force to bring repressed material out of the unconscious and the force to keep repressing the material back into the unconscious. The tension between these two forces resulted in intrapsychic conflict.[7] Even though the patient would resist revealing his repressed experiences, it was through dream analysis and analysis of slips of speech that the person could discover the driving forces behind their adult emotional problems.

Eventually the study of dreams became for Freud "the royal road of the unconscious."[8] His famous book on interpreting dreams (written in 1897) contains an analysis of many of his own dreams over a three-year period. Freud believed that "the sleeper has to dream, because the nightly relaxation of repression allows the upward thrust of the traumatic fixation to become active..."[9] In other words, while sleeping, your mind tries to bring to the conscious part of your mind the memory of the traumas that have been suppressed and are now causing your emotional problems. The psychoanalyst would, in turn, interpret the dreams often concluding they contained symbolic sexual meaning. Freud concluded that neurosis (emotional problems) has a sexual origin (sexual desires toward the parent of the opposite sex and hostile feelings toward the rival parent of the same sex) that begins in infancy. Obviously, sexually desiring one parent and wishing ill will to the other parent would be upsetting, frightening, and guilt-producing to a child. In order to cope, therefore, the child would repress these traumatic memories into his unconscious.

Unfortunately, Sigmund Freud looked into his own sinful heart for answers rather than turning to Scripture. It is well documented that during the years Freud was formulating his famous theories he used cocaine, maintained an avid interest in the occult and numerology, and believed himself destined for fame. Some think that Freud was under the illusion that he was Moses.[10]

Although born a Jew, Freud came to view God as some sort of illusion or wishful thinking. "He called religion the store of ideas 'born from man's need to make his helplessness tolerable and built up from the material of memories of the helplessness of his own childhood...'"[11] In other words, belief in a "personal deity provides an external object on which to project ...[their repressed fear and guilt]"[12] Sigmund Freud was a self-admitted godless man. Tragically he professionalized and legitimized looking inward to a self-deceived heart to find answers rather than looking to Scripture. God, through the prophet Jeremiah, made it clear that only God can accurately search our hearts.

> *The heart is more deceitful than all else and is desperately sick; who can understand it? I, the LORD, search the heart, I test the mind, even to give to each man according to his ways, according to the results of his deeds.* Jeremiah 17:9-10

Our hearts are deceitful and so was Sigmund Freud's. In fact, it was from his spiritually blind heart that Freud thought up his theories. Consider for a moment Freud's various psychoanalytical beliefs and how the Word of God refutes them.

SIGMUND FREUD'S BELIEFS	GOD'S WORD
There is an unconscious part of man that stores painful or threatening memories.	There is no unconscious part of man controlling him. Instead, **"as he thinks within himself, so he is."** **Proverbs 23:7**
Hypnosis is a way to uncover the hidden traumas that are causing emotional problems.	A Christian should only let their mind dwell on **"whatever is true"** (Philippians 4:8). True thoughts conform to reality. There are God-honoring ways to deal with reality even if it is or was traumatic.
Using free association and slips of speech, the patient is prompted by the doctor or allowed to say whatever comes to mind however seemingly unconnected or bizarre it is. Then the doctor interprets it.	The Scripture tells us we are to have control over what we think and say. **"But let everyone be quick to hear, slow to speak and slow to anger;..."** (James 1:19a) **"The heart of the righteous ponders how to answer, but the mouth of the wicked pours out evil things."** (Proverbs 15:28) **"The naive believes everything, but the prudent man considers his steps."** (Proverbs 14:15)
Repression occurs in your mind making the memory of painful or threatening events inaccessible to the conscious mind.	**"For the Word of God is living and active and sharper than any two-edged sword, and piercing as far as the division of soul and spirit, of both joints and marrow, and able to judge the thoughts and intentions of the heart."** (Hebrews 4:12) You cannot delve any deeper inside a person than the "thoughts and intents of their heart" by way of the Word of God.

SIGMUND FREUD'S BELIEFS	GOD'S WORD
Resistance is a defense against painful, repressed memories coming forward into your conscious mind.	Christians are to face reality and biblically deal with traumatic events. If something did happen to you and you were too young to remember it, then simply trust God that He is not going to let something that you do not remember control your life. If something traumatic did happen and you were old enough to remember it, you will remember it. Your responsibility is to forgive and biblically respond. For example, **"pray for those who persecute you" (Matthew 5:44), "overcome evil with good" (Romans 12:21), "do good to those who hate you" (Luke 6:28).**
Dream analysis is thought to be one way to help a patient discover the driving forces behind their adult emotional problems.	**"See to it that no one takes you captive through philosophy and empty deception, according to the tradition of men, according to the elementary principles of the world, rather than according to Christ"** (Colossians 2:8).

Sigmund Freud was spiritually blind and extremely deceived. His beliefs were, at best, bizarre. They are a lost man's attempt to make some sort of sense out of life and emotional problems.

Most modern day psychiatrists, psychologists and Christian psychologists would say they are definitely *not* Freudian because they do not embrace Freud's theory on infant sexuality. However, if the counselor, (like Sue's counselor), makes statements such as "You must get in touch with your pain or feelings," or "You cannot begin to heal until you have gone back into the past and experienced your deepest pain," or "You must uncover those unconscious drives or repressed memories,"or "Something *must* have happened to you as a child. Try to remember," they *are* Freudian in as much as they use many of his theories. The idea of unconscious forces (deep, hidden painful memories) causing one's anxiety, depression, or other emotional problems is simply not true. It is not biblical and it is greatly deceiving Christians today. I do not deny that past traumas affect us and must be biblically addressed, but not in some mystical, secret way.[13]

Abraham Maslow, the second therapist in our brief study, trained under Freud, but proposed a somewhat different view on what causes people to have emotional problems.

Abraham Maslow's Hierarchy of Needs

Maslow lived from 1908 to 1970 and is called the "Father of Modern Psychology." He was an avowed atheist. He did not believe in God or that man is accountable to God. Both Freud and Maslow embraced the concept of an unconscious part of man, but Maslow did not believe it was traumatic infantile sexual identity that was man's problem but, rather, a lack of having one's underlying needs met.

The ultimate goal in Maslow's way of thinking is to be self-actualized. A self-actualized person is confident in himself, feels good about himself, and in turn reaches out to help others. In order to develop this kind of mature personality, his underlying needs must first be met. If his needs are not met, he may experience debilitating emotional pain and problems for an entire lifetime.

Maslow believed that the therapist could usually best help a person progress through the stages towards fulfillment and maturity by placing them in group therapy. Talking about past hurts and traumas and interacting with others would help the hurting person get in touch with their pain and then move past it. Maslow's needs hierarchy looked like this:

Hierarchy of Needs [14]

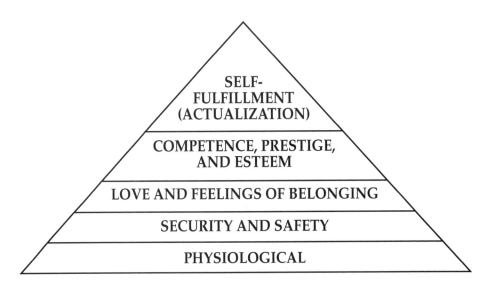

Maslow thought that your underlying needs *(basic physiological needs* for air, water, and food; *basic safety and security needs* such as not having to worry for your life; *basic needs to be loved and feel that you belong and the need to be esteemed)* must be met before you could then become a self-actualized person. *The Harvard Guide of Modern Psychiatry* explains Maslow's theory of personality development as follows:

> The theory of personality developed by Abraham Maslow is a theory of psychic health rather than sickness. It postulates a hierarchy of needs underlying human motivation. When the needs with the greatest potency are satisfied, the next level of needs presses for fulfillment. The hierarchy reaches from the most basic physiological [physical] needs to the highest order of esthetics and spiritual needs.

> For Maslow, man is essentially good. The development and behavior of the individual can only be subverted by the inter-ference of society, which places impediments to the fulfillment of man's inner needs. Particularly important are the needs for esteem, knowledge, and beauty. But social institutions and pro-cesses can also help in the process of self-actualization. The

self-actualized man, who makes full use of his capacities and potentialities, is the central and idealized prototype of Maslow's theory. Such individuals ... are characterized by high levels of objectivity, humility, and creativity, lack of inner conflict, and a capacity for joy.[15]

Because Maslow was an atheist, instead of turning to God's Word to find answers, "in therapy, Maslow aimed at increasing [the patient's] *self*-knowledge and understanding and mobilizing the potentialities and resources of individuals toward greater *self*-actualization. He stressed man's inherent goodness and capacity for love, and he made therapeutic efforts to mobilize these capacities by generating intense, emotional peak experiences."[16]

A Christianized psychological version of a self-actualized man would be described as a mature Christian who is confident of his worth in Christ or who loves himself so that he can, in turn, love others. Certainly, we want all Christians to be mature and to show love to God and others. Believing, however, that your underlying needs must be met before you can mature or overcome emotional problems is not true. It is contrary to Scripture.

Think of the Apostle Paul or the Lord Jesus Christ. How many times were their underlying needs obviously not met? Their lives were often in danger. Certainly many did not love or esteem them. Eventually they were both murdered. The Lord Jesus' death was a slow and torturous one. However, even *during* His horrible crucifixion, Jesus made provisions for his mother's care (John 19:26-27), He forgave those who crucified Him (Luke 23:34), and He forgave and encouraged one of the criminals being crucified beside Him (Luke 23:42-43). Rather than "relieving himself of duty," so to speak, while He died, Jesus continued to give to the others around Him. It is safe to assume that His physical needs certainly were not being met.

We are told repeatedly in the Scriptures to be imitators of Christ (Ephesians 5:2, Philippians 2:5, 1 Peter 2:21, 1 John 2:6). And we know that God will never lead believers into situations that we cannot handle without sinning (1 Corinthians 10:13). So when Maslow theorizes that one's basic needs must be met before he can help others, he is wrong. His theories are contrary to Scripture and to the very example the Lord Jesus Christ gave us to follow. The point being, we can (by God's grace) become a mature person who honors and glorifies God even if no one (now or in the past) esteems, accepts, or loves us.

We frequently hear Maslow's hierarchy of needs "Christianized" through sermons and books that tell us "God loves you, you're special, you're worthy – your *significance* is *in Christ*. If you were the only one, Christ loved you so much He would have died for you. Once you understand that your identity is in

Him, *you* will feel better about *yourself*."

To be "in Christ" means literally to be "in union with Christ." **"...just as He chose us *in* Him before the foundation of the world, that we would be holy and blameless before Him"** (Ephesians 1:4; emphasis added). This is a supernatural union that takes place at the moment of salvation. God does all of the work and seals us together with Him for now and all of eternity (Ephesians 1:13-14). It is not because we *were* so special, worthy, and valuable or because salvation *makes us* so special, so worthy, and so valuable that Christ died for us. Prior to salvation, we were **"dead in our trespasses and sin"** (Ephesians 2:1) and were considered **"enemies of God"** (James 4:4, Romans 5:10). Most likely you were not a mass murderer or baby torturer, but you were nonetheless a sinner.

> *There is none righteous, not even one; there is none who understands, there is no one who seeks for God; all have turned aside, together they have become useless; there is none who does good; there is not even one.*
> *Romans 3:10-12*

Our sin was, and still is, far worse than we realize. *God* is the one who is special and worthy. We should not even think in terms of how wonderful, special, or worthy we are. Certainly all of God's creation, including mankind, is magnificently wonderful because *God*, the Creator, is wonderful. The focus, however, must be on God. Christ died to vindicate "the worth and glory of His Father,"[17] not the worth of sinful man. It is blasphemous and dishonoring to God and Christ's atoning work on the cross to attempt to elevate man to a "Most High" status. Only our holy God is "Most High."

Other Christians incorporate Maslow's hierarchy of needs concept by talking about "self-esteem," wanting to belong, or having a need for "love." They use unbiblical, man-centered terms such as "self-esteem needs," "security needs," "significance needs," or a "filled love cup." They may be like Sue's counselor who concluded that Sue's problems were due to not having her need for love or security met while she was a child. These beliefs are modeled after secular philosophies that only make man more self-centered and self-esteeming than he already is. What this does is entice our sinful flesh to think more and more often and more and more highly of ourselves and what we deserve and less and less highly about God. Ed Welch, in his book, *When Man is Big and God is Small*, makes an excellent point.

> Instead of 'How can I feel better about myself and not be controlled by what people think?' a better question is 'Why am I

so concerned about self-esteem?' or 'Why do I have to have someone – even Jesus – think that I am great?'...we need a way to think less often about ourselves...Regarding other people, our problem is that we need them (for ourselves) more than we love them (for the glory of God). The task God sets for us is to need them less and love them more...ask God what our duty is toward them...the path of service is the road to freedom.[18]

It is plainly wrong to blame our emotional problems on the fact that others do not or did not esteem us or treat us the way we would have like to be treated (or that God would have liked for them to treat us).

In addition to Sigmund Freud's theory of the "unconscious" and Abraham Maslow's "needs" theory, there is another psychologist who has had a major impact on Christian thinking. Erik Erikson's work was in the area of having one's "identity" needs met.

Erik Erickson's Identity Needs

Erik Erikson was an American psychoanalyst who lived from 1902-1994. He studied directly under Abraham Maslow and, like Maslow, was heavily influenced by Sigmund Freud and refers to Freud and his writings often in his book, *Identity, Youth and Crisis.*[19] In his book, Erikson explains how he believes a person develops a healthy, mature personality. He writes of *stages* in the maturing of one's personality. Because Erikson was a firm believer in evolution, he looked on man as some sort of human animal or organism. Thus man must evolve through *stages* in order to become a mature person. "Personality, therefore, can be said to develop according to steps predetermined in the human organism's readiness to be driven toward, to be aware of, and to interact with a widening radius of significant individuals and institutions."[20]

Erikson believed that as the human appproaches a new *stage* in development, he experiences inner conflicts which culminate in a *crisis experience*. If he responds well to the crisis, he will mature to the next level. Erikson explained it this way:

I shall present human growth from the point of view of the conflicts, inner and outer, which the vital personality weathers, re-emerging from each crisis with an increased sense of inner unity, with an increase of good judgment, and an increase in the capacity "to do well" according to his own standards and to the standards of those who are significant to him.[21]

According to Erikson, man must progress through eight stages in his quest for a healthy identity. For example, Erikson believed that an infant within the first year of life had to progress through the *stage* of developing a basic *trust* in people. If they did not, their *mistrust* of others and themselves would result in a life long adult psychopathology.[22]

Another *stage* and time of great inner conflict is the adolescent "identity versus role confusion."[23] Erikson believed that there is "an inevitable conflict that accompanies the growth of a sense of identity in late adolescence."[24] In 1958 he wrote a book entitled *Young Man Luther* in which he explained the so-called identity crisis of the young priest, Martin Luther; hence, Erikson's explanation of the Reformation. In other words, Erikson believed that Luther "rebelled" against the Roman Catholic Church not because Luther became a Christian and saw the error of the church, but because he was trying to find himself!

If the adolescent does not resolve the issue of his identity, he will not move forward through other stages. He will never reach the last and most mature stage which Erikson termed "ego integrity." Within this stage, the aging person accepts their ...

> one and only life cycle and the people who have become significant to it as something that had to be and that, by necessity, permitted of no substitutions. It thus means a new and different love of one's parents, free of the wish that they should have been different, and an acceptance of the fact that one's life is one's own responsibility. It is a sense of comradeship with men and women of distant times and of different pursuits who have created orders and objects and sayings conveying human dignity and love. [25]

A person who does not progress to the "ego integrity" stage will be left in a state of "despair."[26]

Erikson's psychological theory is the basis for what you often hear, that teens must go through a turbulent time of rebellion in their quest to find their own identity. Nowhere in Scripture are we told that this is necessary. In fact, we are told that the teenager (by God's grace) can be very wise and godly and **"have more insight than all [his] teachers"** (Psalm 119:99, adaptation added).

Erikson's theory of personality development is also the Christian Psychologist's model for teaching that your "identity" is *in Christ*. If we can just understand who we are *in Christ*, we will realize our identity and no longer be depressed or anxious or feel badly about ourselves. Sue's counselor (in our earlier example) believed that if Sue could just understand who she is *in Christ*, then she could experience emotional healing. As we said earlier, this is a perversion of the true biblical teaching that Christians are "in Christ." Our union with Christ is a precious truth. We should love it and believe it, but not twist it into something God never intended - a formula to solve emotional problems or make man *feel* worthy.

There are several modern day Christian psychologists who have tried to "Christianize" secular psychological theories. Most of them have adapted a combination of error from Freud, Maslow, and Erikson. No matter how you try to Scripture-coat their counseling beliefs, ultimately you end up with error. It would be like preparing a wonderful cake batter that is clean and pure and then throwing a handful of dirt in it. When you mix the dirt and the cake batter, the batter is contaminated. So, too, is counseling contaminated that is built upon or mixed up with secular psychological beliefs.

Christian Psychologists justify their position by believing that their field is scientific and that their theories are true because "all truth is God's truth." [27] They believe that their theories are included in what is called "general revelation." In other words, they think that anything they regard as scientific "truth" comes under the umbrella of general revelation and is from God. Their belief about general revelation, however, is not accurate since general revelation has only one overall purpose – to reveal God to us (see Psalm 19:1 and Romans 1:18-21).[28] Any study of creation that goes beyond revealing that God exists and is to be feared misuses God's general revelation. So, the problem with how they justify their position is that psychological theories do *not* come under the umbrella of general revelation.

The original purpose of science was (and still should be) to learn more about God's creation so that we can give God more glory. For instance, the more new stars that scientists find, the more reasons we have to be in awe of God and His power. Certainly there are some scientifically observed truths from which we have learned much about God's creation – the earth *is* basically round and orbits around the sun. You will *not* fall off of the earth if you set sail across an ocean. However, what the Christian Psychologists are heralding as truth, under the umbrella of general revelation, is not general revelation and it is not true. Their beliefs are based on godless men's opinions and theories; not scientific truth. Most take psychology, which at best is lost man's way of coping with life, and then try to fit God in where they can. Psychology is the platform from which they operate. Instead, they should be using the very specific content of the Bible in which **"God has given us everything pertaining to life and**

godliness" (2 Peter 1:3). I do not question anyone's sincere desire to help others but many have been sold a bill of goods. They elevate man to a "Most High" status and steal glory from God.

Let me summarize the problems with ...

Psychologized Man

- Psychologized man perceives himself as "needy" in an unbiblical sense. While we desperately do need a personal relationship with God through the Lord Jesus Christ, the focus of this relationship must be on God and what He has done, not on our value or worth. We come to Christ completely unworthy of His cleansing. Our attitude should be one of *"mourning over our sin,"* not "I'm special. I'm valuable. God saved me and gave me worth."   (Matthew 5:3-4)

- Psychologized man believes he is influenced or even controlled by unconscious desires and needs. This is not taught in the Bible and it is not true. We are to be controlled by the Holy Spirit, not some fictional, mystical, unbiblical, unconscious self.
                                      (Galatians 5:16, Ephesians 5:18)

- Psychologized man is focused on self. Often he fears other men or thinks he "needs" others to try to make himself feel better.

- Psychologized man is proud and self-serving. Instead of purely proclaiming *"the excellencies of Him who has called you out of darkness into His marvelous light,"* he proclaims his own value and worth.   (1 Peter 2:9)

- Psychologized man is encouraged to use God for how God can make him feel. Instead, he should repent of his self-focus, deny (him)self, and love others whether he feels like it or not.   (Matthew 22:39)

Psychologized man elevates himself. His focus is inward as he seeks to feel good about himself and have his needs met. As he becomes "Man Most High", he *uses* God instead of *bowing* before God as "God Most High." Like Sue's Christian counselor, he has bought into the philosophies of ungodly men and embraced them as truth. He has been deceived.

Man's emotional problems *cannot* be solved through an inward search, seeking to have his needs met, or realizing who he is (even *in Christ*). Almost all of man's emotional problems *can* be solved by loving God and loving others. In the very few cases where a legitimate physical malady is causing depression or anxiety, doctors can usually treat it. If they cannot, the Christian can, nevertheless, cope with it and not sin against God since **"...God is faithful, who will not allow you to be tempted beyond what you are able..."** (1 Corinthians 10:13).

"Self" is at the center of our lusts – our supposed needs for significance, worth, security, identity, or esteem. A psychologized, man-centered view of God and of man appeals to our natural sense of loving ourselves and thus deceives us. The Christian who is loving God and loving others is outwardly focused. They have turned, by God's grace, from *their* needs and *their* significance to thinking of and proclaiming *God's* worth and *His* significance. They may have problems, but they are not in despair nor are they overwhelmed with fear. Their joy is in the Lord and He is their **"refuge and strength, a very present help in trouble"** (Psalm 46:1).

Now that we have considered who psychologized man is and what is in his heart (how he thinks), we need to bring these issues into our everyday thinking. In order to make certain that you have not been influenced to think about yourself in a psychologized way, take a few minutes and carefully compare the difference in the following chart between "Right Ways to Think" as opposed to "Wrong Ways to Think." Pray that God will make you discerning about these issues.

WRONG WAYS TO THINK	RIGHT WAYS TO THINK
God loves me and because He saw my worth, He saved me. (or) God loves me and saved me and now I have worth.	God does love me and created me in His image. His death on the cross for me shows the depth of my sin. He alone is worthy of praise.
I am in Christ to have my identity needs met. If I would just realize who I am in Christ I would no longer be depressed, have a lack of assurance of salvation, or feel worthless.	Being in Christ is a precious truth. I love thinking about what He has done. I am in Christ for the purpose of proclaiming His excellencies. (1 Peter 2:9)
I want my child to feel good about himself so I am going to tell him how valuable he is and special he is to God.	I love my child and I am going to hug him and tell him so. I'm also going to tell him how grateful I am to God for giving him to us. He is a gift from God. Isn't God good?
God is here to meet my needs to feel worthy or significant.	I am here to serve God and proclaim His excellencies. God use me for your glory!

Conclusion

The so-called "Christian" view of man is changing. It esteems man higher and higher and in the process God gets smaller and smaller. It affects the gospel by making it man-centered instead of God-centered through focusing on man's worth/significance or man's good works. Hence, that gospel is false. It also affects a proper view of sanctification (how people grow and mature as Christians) by turning man's focus on his "needs" and his "identity" instead of his obligation to God. Both the gospel and how we grow as Christians have been perverted by viewing them through a psychologized or false religious lens. Instead of instructing people to repent and assume responsibility for their actions believing that God will give them His grace to help them, this distorted view says to just realize who you are *in Christ* and you will realize your worth and stop struggling with frustration, fear, depression, etc.

The only way we can be freed of our sinful self is to **"know the truth** [as the Lord Jesus said] **and the truth shall make you free"** (John 8:32). The truth is in the Scriptures and in the Person of Jesus Christ. It is not within some secret, hidden, unconscious part of man or man-glorifying twist on what it means to be somebody *in Christ*. We are here to serve and glorify God, not ourselves.

A biblical perspective of man and a pure belief about *God Most High* are not among those issues where good men can agree to disagree. *Please*, prayerfully think this through. In many cases a false gospel is being preached and people are seeking answers to their problems within their own deceived hearts.

What about you? Are you seeking to use God so you can feel better, be happy, and be somebody special or of worth, or are you seeking to glorify Daniel's *"great God Most High?"* How you grow and mature as a Christian is at stake. The destiny of your soul may be at stake. Last and most important of all, the glory and honor of God is at stake.

In the next chapter, we'll see how man's small perception of God does not agree with Daniel's high and lofty view of God.

∞

Chapter 3

Study Questions

1. List the three men in this chapter who have greatly influenced Christian Psychology.

2. Freud believed that there were two basic forces competing in the mind. How did those two forces work against each other?

3. According to Freud, if you have emotional problems what is happening in your mind that is expressed through your dreams?

4. How did Freud view God and religion?

5. According to Jeremiah 17:9-10, what was wrong with Freud looking into his own heart to find answers?

6. In your own words and based on Scripture, what is wrong with the following statements. For help see the chart on pages 31-32.
    a. Man's emotional problems are caused by repressed memories of traumas trying to surface from the unconscious to the conscious mind.

    b. Hypnosis, slips of speech, and dream analysis are good ways for a Psychiatrist to help a patient uncover deep, hidden traumas.

7. What was Abraham Maslow's view of God?

8. What did Maslow think caused men to have emotional problems?

9. According to Maslow, in order to develop a mature personality, what underlying "needs" would have had to have been met?

10. According to the second paragraph on page 35, how would you describe a Christianized version of a self-actualized man?

11. Is Maslow's theory biblical or unbiblical? Why or why not?

12. What does it mean to be "in Christ"? See paragraph one on page 36.

13. What does Christ's death vindicate? See John Piper quote on page 36.

14. What was Erik Erikson's explanation for why Martin Luther "rebelled" against the Roman Catholic Church?

15. Does a Christian teenager have to go through a time of rebellion?

16. What is the purpose of general revelation?

17. Correct the following statements:
    a. "God saved me and gave me worth."

    b. "I am depressed because my underlying needs were not met by my parents."

    c. "I have to love myself before I can love God and others.

    d. "If I just realized who I am in Christ, I would not feel worthless."

    e. "I want my child to have a good self-esteem so I am going to tell him how very special and valuable he is to God."

Chapter 4

Our High and Holy God

Enlighten our minds that we may know Thee as Thou art, so that we may perfectly love Thee and worthily praise Thee.

A.W. Tozer

Modern man has reinvented God. He is comfortable with his new God. Many try to manipulate Him as if He were Santa Claus existing to meet their emotional needs. Psychologized man sees himself as needy, having been wounded emotionally, and driven by unconscious desires and repressed traumas. He is a victim. God is here to serve him and to give him worth. Likewise, Religious man sees himself as the captain of his own fate, thinks he can choose God whenever he pleases, believes himself to be good enough to earn God's favor, and is usually quite pleased with himself. God is also here to serve him.

Unfortunately, psychologized and religious man's God is only a shallow, faint resemblance of Daniel's God Most High. Daniel's God of Heaven is the King and Ruler over His creation. He **"does whatever He pleases"** (Psalm 115:3).

Daniel held to right beliefs about God and His character. In this chapter we will see that Daniel's God is –

- **Sovereign**

- **At Work**

- **Holy**

- **Faithful**

Let's begin with God Most High is sovereign.

God Most High is Sovereign

Sovereignty is the exercise of God's supremacy. In other words, He is the King of kings and the Lord of lords. This fact simply means that God is the Ruler. He is in control. He rules (whether we like it or not). There is no such thing as Mother Nature, but there are *acts of God*. As His creatures, our responsibility is to graciously bow to His authority. Think about the following biblical principles concerning God's sovereignty:

1. God is subject to no one.

    > *...this I [Paul] proclaim to you. "The God who made the world and all things in it, since He is Lord of heaven and earth, does not dwell in temples made with hands; neither is He served by human hands, as though He needed anything, since He Himself gives to all people life and breath and all things..."*
    >
    > *Acts 17:24-25, explanation added*

2. God rules over all.

    > *The LORD has established His throne in the heavens, and His sovereignty rules over all.*
    >
    > *Psalm 103:19*

3. God's rule is good news, a welcome relief for those who know Him.

    > *How lovely on the mountains are the feet of him who brings <u>good news</u>, who announces peace and brings good news of happiness, who announces salvation, and says to Zion, "<u>Your God reigns</u>!"*
    >
    > *Isaiah 52:7, emphasis added*

4. God gives a strong warning for those who do not know God or bow before Him.

    > *Now therefore, O kings, show discernment; take warning, O judges of the earth. Worship the LORD with reverence and rejoice with trembling. Do homage to the Son,*

*lest He become angry, and you perish in the way, for His
wrath may soon be kindled. How blessed are all who take
refuge in Him!*   **Psalm 2:10-12**

5. God does as He pleases.

*For I know that the LORD is great and that our Lord is
above all gods. Whatever the LORD pleases, He does, in
heaven and in earth, in the seas and in all deeps.*
                                              Psalm 135:5-6

6. God (the Lord Jesus Christ) is the head over all authorities.

*...and in Him [the Lord Jesus Christ] you have been made
complete, and He is the head over all rule and authority...*   **Colossians 2:10, explanation added**

7. God makes choices and we have no right to criticize Him.

*I am the LORD, and there is no other; besides Me there is
no God. I will gird you, though you have not known Me;
that men may know from the rising to the setting of the
sun that there is no one besides Me. I am the LORD and
there is no other, The One forming light and creating darkness, causing well-being and creating calamity; I am the
LORD who does all these things. Drip down, O heavens,
from above, and let the clouds pour down righteousness;
Let the earth open up and salvation bear fruit, and righteousness spring up with it. I, the LORD, have created it.
Woe to the one who quarrels with his Maker – an earth-
enware vessel among the vessels of earth! Will the clay
say to the potter, "What are you doing?" or the thing you
are making say, "He has no hands?"*
                              Isaiah 45:5-9, emphasis added

Because God is God and supreme ruler over all His creation, He decides
what His creatures may and may not do. For instance, God gave permission for
Adam to eat all of the fruit in the garden of Eden except for one tree (Genesis
3:2-3). He commanded the Israelites to drive out the Canaanites from the promised land (Joshua 17:18). It is God who determined the role of the wife and how

she may best glorify Him through righteous, gracious submission to her husband (Ephesians 5:22-24). God set the standards. He has determined what is sin and what is righteousness. Only He can know what particular tests or trials are best suited for us to become holy and to have special opportunities to glorify Him (James 1:2-3). God also chooses those for salvation whom He pleases and His choice is based on no merit of our own as **"...He has mercy on whom He desires, and He hardens whom He desires"** (Romans 9:18).

Some of God's creatures have a love/hate view of God's rule. When life is going their way, they love it. When life is not going their way, they hate it. Charles Spurgeon expressed this eloquently:

> Men will allow God to be everywhere except on His throne. They will allow Him in His workshop to fashion worlds and stars...to dispense His bounties...to sustain the earth and bear up pillars of light...but when God ascends His throne, His creatures then gnash their teeth...for God on His throne is not the God they love.

God rules over His creation. This thought is a comfort and joy for those who are persuaded of God's goodness. This thought is terrifying and distressing, however, for those who are not. God not only rules over His creation, but He is actively working in His creation.

God Most High is at Work

God does not take a hands off and "let's see what they will do" view of His creation. He is not present in the sense that we can see Him, but He is nonetheless ever present and working in His creation. Think about the following verses that show ways in which God is currently working.

1. God's work is displayed through His creation.

> *By the seventh day God completed His work which He had done, and He rested on the seventh day from all His <u>work which He had done</u>.*
> *Genesis 2:2, emphasis added*

> *The heavens are telling of the glory of God; and their expanse is <u>declaring the work of His hands</u>.*
> *Psalm 19:1, emphasis added*

2. God continues to work in His creation.

> *He established the earth upon its foundations, so that it will not totter forever and ever...He sends forth springs in the valleys; they flow between the mountains; they give drink to every beast of the field; the wild donkeys quench their thirst. Beside them the birds of the heavens dwell; they lift up their voices among the branches. He waters the mountains from His upper chambers; the earth is satisfied with the fruit of His works. He causes the grass to grow for the cattle, and vegetation for the labor of man, so that he may bring forth food from the earth, and wine which makes man's heart glad, so that he may make his face glisten with oil, and food which sustains man's hearts. The trees of the LORD drink their fill, the cedars of Lebanon which He planted, where the birds build their nests, and the stork, whose home is the fir trees. The high mountains are for the wild goats; the cliffs are a refuge for the rock badgers. He made the moon for the seasons; the sun knows the place of its setting. You appoint darkness and it becomes night, in which all the beasts of the forest prowl about. The young lions roar after their prey and seek their food from God. When the sun rises they withdraw and lie down in their dens. Man goes forth to his work and to his labor until evening. O LORD, <u>how many are Your works</u>! In wisdom You have made them all; the earth is full of Your possessions.*
>
> *Psalm 104: 5, 10-24, emphasis added*

3. God delights in working in His creation through exercising His loving-kindness, justice, and righteousness on earth.

> *Thus says the LORD, "Let not a wise man boast of his wisdom, and let not the mighty man boast of his might, let not a rich man boast of his riches; but let him who boasts boast of this, that he understands and knows Me, that I am the LORD who exercises lovingkindness, justice and righteousness on earth; <u>for I delight in these things</u>," declares the LORD.*
>
> *Jeremiah 9:23-24, emphasis added*

4. The Lord Jesus Christ came to earth to accomplish the work of salvation for sinful man.

    > *These things Jesus spoke; and lifting up His eyes to heaven, He said, "Father, the hour has come; glorify Your Son, that the Son may glorify You, even as You gave Him authority over all flesh, that to all whom You have given Him, He may give eternal life. This is eternal life, that they may know You, the only true God, and Jesus Christ whom You have sent. I glorified You on the earth, <u>having accomplished the work which You have given Me to do</u>."*
    > *John 17:1-4, emphasis added*

5. God uses circumstances in our life to work for our good.

    > *And we know that God causes <u>all things to work together for good to</u> those who love God, to those who are called according to His purpose.*
    > *Romans 8:28, emphasis added*

6. God is working now to mature believers.

    > *For I am confident of this very thing, that He who <u>began a good work in you</u> will perfect it until the day of Christ Jesus.*   *Philippians 1:6, emphasis added*

    > *...for it is God <u>who is at work in you</u>, both to will and to work for His good pleasure.*
    > *Philippians 2:13, emphasis added*

From the beginning of time (which God created) until now, God continues to work in His creation. Two thousand years ago, He sent His beloved Son, the Lord Jesus Christ, to accomplish the work of salvation for all those who would believe. Because of that work, He is still drawing believers to Himself, saving them, and maturing them into Christlikeness. This is really the only rational worldview that bestows on God His proper position – that of "God Most High." It is also the only worldview that provides man his proper position and appropriate outlook on life – that of man created in the image of God for His glory.

> Some knowledge of what kind of God it is that operates the universe is indispensable to a sound philosophy of life and a sane outlook on the world scene.
> A.W. Tozer[29]

So far we have seen that God Most High is ruling His creation and working in His creation. Fortunately for us, He has only perfectly pure actions and motives. Our God is a holy God.

God Most High is Holy

The holiness of God means that His essential nature is pure and without sin. Holiness refers either to God Himself or to what has been made holy by Him. The holiness of God should evoke great wonder and praise from His creatures. On one hand it is a relief to us that God cannot sinfully rule, but on the other hand it is frightening because He demands perfection of His creatures. His standard is unattainable by man apart from God's cleansing work on our behalf. In fact, there is nothing more terrifying than to be in the presence of the holiness of God. Before Adam and Eve sinned, they did not dread God (Genesis 3:8). After they sinned, they hid from God. Now when man is confronted with God's holiness, he is afraid because he sees his own sin (Isaiah 6:1-5). The holiness of God is a biblical concept that is well established throughout the Scriptures. Consider the following Scriptural principles concerning the holiness of God.

1. God is holy. He is set apart, sacred, and pure.

    > *Your [God's] eyes are <u>too pure to approve evil</u>, and You cannot look on wickedness with favor.*
    > *Habakkuk 1:13, explanation and emphasis added*

    > *God reigns over the nations, God sits on <u>His holy throne</u>.*
    > *Psalm 47:8, emphasis added*

2. God's holiness is the very excellency of His Divine nature.[30]

    > *In the year of King Uzziah's death I [Isaiah] saw the Lord sitting on a throne, lofty and exalted, with the train of His robe filling the temple. Seraphim stood above Him, each having six wings: with two he covered his face, and with two he covered his feet, and with two he flew. And one called out to another and said, "<u>Holy, Holy, Holy, is the LORD of hosts, the whole earth is full of His glory</u>." And the foundations of the thresholds trembled at the voice of him who called out, while the temple was filling with smoke. Then I [Isaiah] said, "Woe is me, for I am ruined! Because I am a man of unclean lips, and I live*

> *among a people of unclean lips; for my eyes have seen the King, the LORD of hosts."*
> *Isaiah 6:1-5, explanation and emphasis added*

3. As children of God, we are to be holy as He is holy.

> *As obedient children, do not be conformed to the former lusts which were yours in your ignorance, but <u>like the Holy One who called you</u>, be holy yourselves also in all your behavior; because it is written, "YOU SHALL BE HOLY, FOR I AM HOLY."*
> *1 Peter 1:14-16, emphasis added*

4. Only a holy God/Man could redeem sinful man from his sin.

> *He [God] made Him [the Lord Jesus Christ] who knew no sin to be sin on our behalf, so that we might become the righteousness of God in Him.*
> *2 Corinthians 5:21, explanation added*

God is *pure* and so holy that He has to punish sin. It is clear from Scripture that He **"will by no means leave the guilty unpunished"** (Nahum 1:3). God satisfied His wrath against sin when He condescended to become a man and died on the cross. Man himself cannot ever satisfy God's holy demands (no matter how hard he tries) because each man sins and thus deserves his own punishment. Only Christ (God in the flesh) could possibly have satisfied the wrath of God (1 John 2:2). Christ perfectly obeyed all of God's Laws. He was pure and innocent of all sin and did not deserve death or punishment. In other words, He took the punishment that we deserve. Because Christ was innocent, God was satisfied and those *in Christ* are forgiven.

Often you hear someone use Adolf Hitler as the worst example of a wicked, evil person one could imagine. Certainly we would not consider ourselves to be that bad. Listen to what R.C. Sproul wrote about Hitler, our own sin, and the holiness of God.

> We have more in common with Adolf Hitler than we do with God. Because we sin, we are all guilty of treason against our Creator. The gap between you and God is [infinite]... We take God's mercy for granted. Our hearts have become callous and we demand it. God is not obliged to be merciful... He is [obliged] to vindicate His holiness and be just. He has the freedom to

show mercy or justice. I can understand His justice. His mercy staggers my imagination. Only once in History has an innocent man suffered - the highest possible expression of mercy happened for you.[31]

God is Holy. He rules and works in His creation. He also is faithful.

God Most High is Faithful

How many times have you sung the hymn *Great Is Thy Faithfulness?* How many times have you really meant what you were singing? Faithfulness is that attribute of God that causes Him to be completely trustworthy to fulfill His promises and keep His Word. It is because of God's faithfulness that we can have complete confidence in God and His Word. It thrills my soul to think of God's promises such as the one the Lord Jesus made when He said, **"Because I live, you can live also"** (John 14:19). He *will* raise us from the dead. He *will* reward us for our good works (1 Corinthians 3:14). He *will* punish unbelievers (Revelation 20:11-15). God Most High is faithful.

1. God is faithful to keep His Word.

   God is not a man, that He should lie, nor a son of man, that He should repent; has He said, and will He not do it? Or has He spoken, and will He not make it good?
   Numbers 23:19

   If we are faithless, He [God] remains faithful, for He cannot deny Himself.   2 Timothy 2:13, explanation added

2. God's faithfulness is unlimited.

   Your lovingkindness, O LORD, extends to the heavens, Your faithfulness reaches to the skies.
   Psalm 36:5

3. God's faithfulness is great!

   The LORD's lovingkindnesses indeed never cease, for His compassions never fail. They are new every morning; great is Your faithfulness.
   Lamentations 3:22-23, emphasis added

4. God's faithfulness is illustrated in keeping His promise to deliver the children of Israel from bondage in Egypt.

> *The LORD did not set His love on you nor choose you because you were more in number than any of the peoples, for you were the fewest of all peoples, but because the LORD loved you and kept the oath which He swore to your forefathers, the LORD brought you out by a mighty hand and redeemed you from the house of slavery, from the hand of Pharaoh king of Egypt. Know therefore that the LORD your God, He is God, the faithful God, who keeps His covenant and His lovingkindness to a thousandth generation with those who love Him and keep His commandments; ...*   *Deuteronomy 7:7-9*

5. God is faithful in calling His people.

> *God is faithful, through whom you were called into fellowship with His Son, Jesus Christ our Lord.*
>   *1 Corinthians 1:9*

6. God is faithful to not allow us to be tempted beyond what we are able to bear.

> *No temptation has overtaken you but such as is common to man; and God is faithful, who will not allow you to be tempted beyond what you are able, but with the temptation will provide the way of escape also, so that you will be able to endure it.*
>   *1 Corinthians 10:13*

7. God is faithful to forgive the sin that we confess.

> *If we confess our sins, He is faithful and righteous to forgive us our sins and to cleanse us from all unrighteousness.*   *1 John 1:9*

8. God is faithful even when He afflicts us.

> *I know, O LORD, that Your judgments are righteous, and that in faithfulness You have afflicted me.*
>   *Psalm 119:75, emphasis added*

9. We should accept God as faithful and act upon that knowledge.

   Let us hold fast the confession of our hope without wavering, for He who promised is faithful...

   Hebrews 10:23

10. God is faithful and we should entrust our souls to Him even amid suffering.

    Therefore, let those also who suffer according to the will of God entrust their souls to a faithful Creator in doing what is right.

    1 Peter 4:19

God is faithful to keep His promises. We *can* entrust our souls to Him whether suffering or dying. When we confess our sin, because of His faithfulness, He remains ever ready to forgive and cleanse us (1 John 1:9). "God is faithful and that knowledge should stop our murmurings against Him. He is *greatly honored when we have good thoughts of Him* even in trials and chastening."[32]

Conclusion

God will forever remain true to His character – sovereign, working in His creation, holy, and faithful. Holding to right beliefs about God means viewing Him as He is revealed to us through the Scriptures. That means seeing God as Daniel did – God Most High. Assuming that you embrace a high view of God, what, then, is your responsibility?

A HIGH VIEW OF GOD	YOUR RESPONSIBILITY
For the LORD Most High is to be feared, a great King over all the earth. Psalm 47:2	To have a reverential fear of God. **Charm is deceitful and beauty is vain but a woman who fears the Lord, she shall be praised.** **Proverbs 31:30**
And they remembered that God was their rock and the Most High God their Redeemer. **Psalm 78:35**	Live your life reverently, remembering that God redeemed you from your sin. **If you address as Father the One who impartially judges according to each one's work, conduct yourselves in fear during the time of your stay on earth; knowing that you were not redeemed with perishable things like silver or gold from your futile way of life inherited from your forefather, but with precious blood, as of a lamb unblemished and spotless, the blood of Christ. 1 Peter 1:17-19**
That they may know that You alone, whose name is the LORD, are the Most High over all the earth. Psalm 83:18	Bow before God as Most High over all the earth. You are His creature here to serve Him. He is the Lord. He alone is Most High. You are to submit to His will whether you feel like it or not. **But now, O LORD, You are our Father, we are the clay and You our potter; and all of us are the work of Your hand. Isaiah 64:8**

I will give thanks to the LORD according to His righteousness and will sing praises to the name of the LORD Most High. Psalm 7:17	Sing praises and give thanks to the LORD Most High. Let the word of Christ richly dwell within you, with all wisdom teaching and admonishing one another with psalms and hymns and spiritual songs, singing with thankfulness in your hearts to God. Colossians 3:16
For thus says the high and exalted One who lives forever, whose name is Holy, "I dwell on a high and holy place, and also with the contrite and lowly of spirit. In order to revive the spirit of the lowly and to revive the heart of the contrite. Isaiah 57:15	Realize that it is a miracle of God's grace that He stoops to save us. For by grace you have been saved through faith; and that not of yourselves, it is the gift of God; not as a result of works, so that no one may boast. Ephesians 2:8-9
Behold, My servant [the Messiah to come] will prosper. He will be high and lifted up, and greatly exalted. Isaiah 52:13, explanation added	Look forward and be ready for the day when the Lord Jesus will be exalted by all as He should. Therefore also God highly exalted Him, and bestowed on Him the name which is above every name, that at the name of Jesus every knee should bow, of those who are in heaven, and on earth, and under the earth, and that every tongue should confess that Jesus Christ is Lord, to the glory of God the Father. Philippians 2:9-11

I will cry to God Most High, to God who accomplishes all things for me. **Psalm 57:2**	Trust God to accomplish what you could never accomplish by yourself. **Faithful is He who calls you, and He also will bring it to pass.** **1 Thessalonians 5:24**

Because God is the supreme Ruler of His creation, is working in His creation, is holy and pure, and faithful to keep His promises, we have a responsibility to worship Him as He deserves. Realize that God Most High is not your peer, pal, buddy, or friend in the sense of a chum. We are to serve Him, not use Him to serve us. Bow before Him and tell of *His worth*. Praise *Him* for His works and attributes. Give honor to Him as you study His Word. Treat Him with the utmost care. Do not be trite with Him. Many people reduce Him to the marketing level of Elvis Presley or Mickey Mouse. Instead, express deep gratitude as a constant attitude by delighting in Him and thanking Him every day, all day no matter your circumstances or trials. Never take His atoning work on the cross and His abiding presence for granted.

As creatures of Daniel's God Most High, we must remember who we are and who He is.

GOD IS	**WE ARE HIS**
Lord	Servant
Master	Slave
King	Subject
Creator	Creature
Potter	Clay
God	Man
Redeemer	Redeemed
Bridegroom	Bride

In this chapter we have seen a glimpse of God Most High. In the next chapter, we will see in much more depth God's High and Holy Standard for His creatures. Daniel's God *is* Most High and Holy. Your view of God should be one and the same. Won't you pray and ask God to give you a renewed heart to revere Him and honor Him just as Daniel did?

For **He alone** is worthy.

∞

Chapter 4

Study Questions

1. What does it mean that God is sovereign?

2. Answer the following questions from the biblical principles on God's sovereignty:
   a. According to Acts 17:24-25, what does God need?

   b. According to Psalm 103:19, where is God's throne? How far-reaching is His rule?

   c. According to Isaiah 52:7, how do those who know the Lord view His rule over them?

   d. According to Psalm 2:10-12, what is the warning to the kings of the earth?

e. According to Psalm 135:5-6, who is the LORD above? What does He do?

f. According to Colossians 2:10, whom is the Lord Jesus Christ head over?

g. According to Isaiah 45:5-9, why do we have no right to criticize the choices that God makes?

3. What is wrong with the following statements?
   a. It was not fair when God told Adam he could not eat the fruit of <u>all</u> of the trees in the garden.

   b. The role of the wife is determined by the customs of the day. Therefore, it changes over time.

   c. God has compassion for us when we undergo trials, but He is powerless to prevent them.

   d. God has mercy on those who do good works.

4. From the biblical principles on God's work, answer the following questions:

    a. According to Psalm 19:1 and Genesis 2:2, through what is God's work displayed?

    b. According to Psalm 104, what are some examples of how God continues to work in His creation?

    c. According to Jeremiah 9:23-24, what kind of boasting does the Lord delight in?

    d. According to John 17:1-4, what "work" did the Lord Jesus accomplish?

    e. According to Romans 8:28, if we love God, how does God use circumstances in our lives?

    f. According to Philippians 1:6 and 2:13, how is God working in the life of believers?

5. What is wrong with the following statements?

a. God is working in the lives of Christians to show them how truly significant they are.

b. God worked in His creation and got it going. Now He takes a "hands off" approach.

6. Why did Adam and Eve hide from God?

7. Answer the following questions based on the biblical principles concerning the holiness of God:
   a. According to Habakkuk 1:13, what is God too pure to do?

   b. According to Isaiah 6:1-5, what was Isaiah's reaction when he saw the Lord on His throne in the Temple?

   c. According to 1 Peter 1:14-16, in what way are we to be holy? Why are we to be holy?

   d. Based on 2 Corinthians 5:21, how is it that we (as sinners) can have a relationship with God who is holy?

8. What is wrong with the following statements?
   a. If a man tries hard enough, God will be satisfied that he is good enough to go to heaven.

   b. All people are forgiven by God as long as they are sincere in their religion.

9. From the biblical principles on God's faithfulness answer the following questions:
   a. According to 2 Timothy 2:13, why does God remain faithful even if we are faithless?

   b. According to Psalm 36:5, how far does God's faithfulness reach?

   c. According to Lamentations 3:22-23, what one word did Jeremiah use to describe God's faithfulness?

   d. According to Deuteronomy 7:7-9, how was God's faithfulness shown?

e. According to Hebrews 10:23, on what basis are we told to hold fast to our "confession of hope"?

f. Make a list of ways God is faithful using the following Scripture: 1 Corinthians 1:9; 1 Corinthians 10:13; 1 John 1:9; Psalm 119:75; 1 Peter 4:19.

10. What is wrong with the following statements?
    a. God understands when we grumble and complain if we are having a difficult time.

    b. God's role in your life is to do whatever it takes to make you happy.

    c. If you believe in yourself there is nothing that you cannot accomplish.

Chapter 5

God's High and Holy Standard

He just "crossed the line!" You may have said that to yourself concerning your child who is misbehaving. Or perhaps you have tolerated a neighbor's loud, noisy parties until one night when there were partygoers out in *your* yard making loud revelry outside *your* window. You call the police because by coming into your yard, they have "crossed the line." This "line" that you set is arbitrary. What one neighbor or parent would tolerate another may not.

I have found that Christians have a "line" that they will not cross regarding their sin against God. Most of us would not rob a bank or have an abortion. Most would not commit adultery or take illegal drugs. Most would never even think of going on a drinking binge until they passed out on the floor. Yes, unfortunately there *is* a line that we will not cross regarding sin. The reason I say "unfortunately" is because there *are* sins that *we will* commit as long as we do not cross the "line" of our own standard. God's standard, however, is far more pure and holy than ours. He also has a line, but it is not arbitrary. It is the straight edge of His Law. *All* sin crosses His line, not just the big ones. It is not all right with God for us to *not* commit adultery but *to* gossip. Neither is it acceptable for us to *not* get drunk but *to* worry.

God's standard is not arbitrary, nor is it graded on a scale. It is completely pure and righteous. *All* that we do or think (including everyday, mundane actions such as eating or drinking) is to be done exclusively for the glory of God Most High. God is the King of glory. He is (because of who He is and what He has done) worthy of all honor and praise. To glorify God means to call attention to His worth and to proclaim His excellencies. We are to do this as we are to love Him — with all our heart. God's glory should be our supreme delight and is our highest good. It should be something that we seek and greatly desire.

For example, we give God glory when we are delighted to uphold His high and holy standards. In this chapter we will consider some of those standards as we look at thirteen biblical aspects of glorifying God. Under each point, I will ask you questions and give Scripture for you to ponder soberly. As Christians we all talk about giving God glory, but often we do not. Before you read on, please pray and ask God to convict you and teach you.

Thirteen Biblical Ways to Glorify God

(Adapted from material by my pastor, John Crotts, and Thomas Watson, a seventeenth century Puritan pastor)[33]

1. Aim your life exclusively at God's glory.

> *For not one of us lives for himself, and not one dies for himself; for if we live, we live for the Lord, or if we die, we die for the Lord; therefore whether we live or die, we are the Lord's.* **Romans 14:7-8**

> *...but that with all boldness, Christ will even now, as always, be exalted in my body, whether by life or by death. For to me, to live is Christ and to die is gain.* **Philippians 1:20-21**

> *Whether, then, you eat or drink or whatever you do, do all to the glory of God.* **1 Corinthians 10:31**

Questions:
- Do you prefer God's glory above all other things?
- Are you content that God's will should take place even though yours does not?
- Are you content to be outshined by others as long as God is glorified?
- Are you tenderly concerned that God is glorified in all of life? Your relationship with your husband? The elders in the church? Your family and friends? Your secret thoughts?
- Are you hurt when God and His Word are dishonored?

2. Worship the God of Glory.

> *When the priests came forth from the holy place...and all the Levitical singers...clothed in fine linen, with cymbals, harps and lyres, standing east of the altar, and with them one hundred and twenty priests blowing trumpets in unison when the trumpeters and the singers were to make themselves heard with one voice to praise and to glorify the LORD, and when they lifted up their voice accompanied by trumpets and cymbals and instruments of music, and when they praised the LORD saying, "He indeed is good for His lovingkindess is everlasting," then the house, the house of the LORD, was filled with a cloud, so that the priests could not stand to minister because of the cloud, for the glory of the LORD filled the house of God...*
> *2 Chronicles 5:11-14*

> *All nations which you have made shall come and worship before You, O Lord, and they shall glorify Your name. For You are great and do wondrous deeds; You alone are God. Teach me Your way, O LORD; I will walk in your truth; Unite my heart to fear Your name. I will give thanks to You, O LORD my God, with all my heart, and will glorify Your name forever. For Your lovingkindness toward me is great, and You have delivered my soul from the depths of Sheol.*
> *Psalm 86:9-13*

Questions:

- Do you think about the words of hymns and truly sing them to the Lord?
- Do you bow before Him, acknowledging Him as God and you as His creature?
- Do you affirm in your heart teaching from God's Word?
- Do you concentrate on what the pastor is preaching/teaching?
- Do you concentrate on the Lord and what He has done? Or does your mind wander to yourself and other cares?
- Do you have a reverential awe of God? Are you respectful to Him?

3.   Sincerely confess your sins.

> *Blessed are those who mourn [over their sin and its effects], for they shall be comforted.*
> *Matthew 5:4, explanation added*

> *If we confess our sins, He is faithful and righteous to forgive us our sins and to cleanse us from all unrighteousness.*   *1 John 1:9*

> *He who conceals his transgressions will not prosper, but he who confesses and forsakes them will find compassion.*   *Proverbs 28:13*

> *For what I am doing, I do not understand; for I am not practicing what I would like to do, but I am doing the very thing I hate...Wretched man that I am! Who will set me free from the body of this death? Thanks be to God through Jesus Christ our Lord! So then, on the one hand I myself with my mind am serving the law of God, but on the other, with my flesh the law of sin.*
> *Romans 7:15,24-25*

Questions:
- Do you find yourself sinning less and less, but being more and more grieved over sins you do commit?
- Are you willing to do whatever it takes to turn from sin even if it includes seeking accountability?
- Are you deeply ashamed of past sin, yet honor God by believing His Word that tells you if you are a Christian you are forgiven?
- Do you exalt God by taking sin against Him seriously?

4.   Believe in Him for salvation and throughout your life.

> *The one who believes in the Son of God has the witness in himself; the one who does not believe God has made Him a liar, because he has not believed in the witness that God has given concerning His Son. And the witness is this, that God has given us eternal life, and this life is in His Son.*   *1 John 5:10-11*

...yet, with respect to the promise of God, he [Abraham] did not waver in unbelief but grew strong in faith, giving glory to God, and being fully assured that what God had promised, He was able also to perform.
   Romans 4:20-21, explanation added, emphasis added

Trust in the LORD with all your heart and do not lean on your own understanding.   Proverbs 3:5

Questions:

- Do you trust God with your life and your loved ones?

- Do you believe that He is good?

- Have you thought about death and how you can trust Him to take you through it?

- Do you realize that the presence of God and the truth of His Word is reality even if it goes against how you feel or what you can see?

5.   Give God glory through bearing fruit for Him.

By this is My Father glorified, that you bear much fruit, and so prove to be My disciples.   John 15:8

Let your light shine before men in such a way that they may see your good works, and glorify your Father who is in heaven.   Matthew 5:16

Questions:

- Is doing what God wants you to do more important than what you want to do?

- Are you willing to obey God even if it means biblically exposing a family member's sin?

- Can you honestly sing the chorus, "Oh, How I Love Jesus," and mean it because you are being obedient to His Word?

- Are you faithfully obedient even when you would rather be doing something else?

- Do you do your work heartily (however boring or seemingly unspiritual) as unto the Lord?

- Are you obedient even in your thoughts?

- Are you just as obedient at home as you are in public?

6. Cultivate grateful contentment wherever God has placed you.

> *Not that I speak from want, for I have learned to be content in whatever circumstances I am.*
>
> *Philippians 4:11*

> *Concerning this [Paul's thorn in the flesh] I implored the Lord three times that it might leave me. And He has said to me, "My grace is sufficient for you, for power is perfected in weakness." Most gladly, therefore, I will rather boast about my weaknesses, so that the power of Christ may dwell in me. Therefore I am well content with weaknesses, with insults, with distresses, with persecutions, with difficulties, for Christ's sake; for when I am weak, then I am strong.*
>
> *2 Corinthians 12:8-10, explanation added*

Questions:

- Do you truly desire to glorify God even if it means physical or emotional pain for you or a loved one?

- Do you pray that God will use you for His glory whatever that means?

- Do you believe that God is the only one who can know how you can glorify Him the most?

- Will you stay single or stay married and rejoice in what God is doing because that is God's will for you at the moment?

- Is your first thought to thank God when a trial is suddenly thrust upon you?

- Do you feel sorry for yourself if things do not turn out the way you hoped?

7. Grow spiritually.

> *You therefore, beloved, knowing this beforehand, be on your guard so that you are not carried away by the error of unprincipled men and fall from your own steadfastness, but grow in the grace and knowledge of our Lord and Savior Jesus Christ.*　*2 Peter 3:17-18*

> *But we all, with unveiled face, beholding as in a mirror the glory of the Lord, are being transformed into the same image from glory to glory, just as from the Lord, the Spirit.*　*2 Corinthians 3:18*

> *... like newborn babies, long for the pure milk of the word, so that by it you may grow in respect to salvation ...*　*1 Peter 2:2*

Questions:

- Does your life show others what God's power can do?
- Can you look back over your years as a Christian and see growth?
- Do you long to grow more and more like the Lord Jesus or are you content to rest on the past?
- Would unbelievers who know you say that you are changing?
- Do you deeply desire God's Word?
- Do you want God to show you your sin and to prune you even if you must suffer embarrassment in the process or admit that you were wrong?

8. Stand up for God's truth.

> **Beloved, while I was making every effort to write you about our common salvation, I felt the necessity to write to you appealing that you contend earnestly for the faith which was once for all delivered to the saints.**　**Jude 3**

> For whoever is ashamed of Me and My words in this
> adulterous and sinful generation, the Son of Man will
> also be ashamed of him when He comes in the glory of
> His Father with the holy angels.   Mark 8:38

Questions:

- Do you speak up regarding God's truth or are you like the person who says, "I have faith, but it is private?"

- Do you study the Scriptures diligently so that you will know where to look to find key passages or are you unable to find passages without asking for help?

- When you do confront error, is it done in love with a gentle tone of voice or is it done in sinful pride to prove that you are right?

- Are you more concerned with standing up for God's truth or with what others might think of you? Whom do you really desire to glorify?

- Do you see God's truth as a precious treasure to be carefully protected lest others take from it?

9. Cultivate zeal for His name. Zeal is a mixture of love and anger - an intense love for God and anger at sin.

> I know your deeds and your toil and perseverance, and
> that you cannot tolerate evil men, and you put to the
> test those who call themselves apostles, and they are
> not, and you found them to be false; and you have per-
> severance and have endured for My name's sake, and
> have not grown weary.   Revelation 2:2-3

> And He found in the temple those who were selling
> oxen and sheep and doves, and the money changers
> seated at their tables. And He made a scourge of cords,
> and drove them all out of the temple, with the sheep
> and the oxen; and He poured out the coins of the money
> changers and overturned their tables; and to those who
> were selling the doves He said, "Take these things away;
> stop making My Father's house a house of merchan-

dise." His disciples remembered that it was written, "ZEAL FOR YOUR HOUSE WILL CONSUME ME."
John 2:14-17

Questions:

- Would people say of you, "She is sincere in her faith"?

- Do you grieve when you know of churches that have an outward form of religion but deny or compromise the truth?

- When someone uses the Lord's name in vain, is it your heart's desire to speak up and say something like, "Please, don't do that. God's name is very precious and we are to speak of Him in a respectful way."

- Are you passionate in your love for God?

- Do you pray and ask God to grant people repentance because you want Him to be glorified in their lives?

10. Witness to the lost.

> Go therefore and make disciples of all the nations, baptizing them in the name of the Father and the Son and the Holy Spirit, teaching them to observe all that I commanded you; and lo, I am with you always, even to the end of the age.
> Matthew 28:19-20

> But even if you should suffer for the sake of righteousness, you are blessed. AND DO NOT FEAR THEIR INTIMIDATION, AND DO NOT BE TROUBLED, but sanctify Christ as Lord in your hearts, <u>always being ready to make a defense to everyone who asks you to give an account for the hope that is in you,</u> yet with gentleness and reverence...
> 1 Peter 3:14-15, emphasis added

> Therefore, we are ambassadors for Christ, as though God were entreating through us; we beg you on behalf of Christ, be reconciled to God.
> 2 Corinthians 5:20

Questions:

- Can you give (at a moment's notice) a good, clear, God-honoring gospel presentation? Can you readily find verses?

- Do you look for ways to turn a conversation towards the gospel?

- Do you understand that you are not responsible for whether or not the person believes in the Lord Jesus, but that you are responsible to present the claims of Christ hoping God might grant them faith in Him?

11. Be willing to suffer or die for God.

> *Beloved, do not be surprised at the fiery ordeal among you, which comes upon you for your testing, as though some strange thing were happening to you; but to the degree that you share the sufferings of Christ, keep on rejoicing, so that also at the revelation of His glory you may rejoice with exultation. If you are reviled for the name of Christ, you are blessed, because the Spirit of glory and of God rests on you. Make sure that none of you suffers as a murderer, or thief, or evildoer, or a troublesome meddler; but if anyone suffers as a Christian, he is not to be ashamed, but is to glorify God in this name.*
> *1 Peter 4:12-16*

> *For I consider that the sufferings of this present time are not worthy to be compared with the glory that is to be revealed to us.* *Romans 8:18*

> *...that I may know Him and the power of His resurrection and the fellowship of His sufferings, being conformed to His death...* *Philippians 3:10*

Questions:

- Do you believe that the Lord Jesus is worth dying for?
- Would you consider it a privilege to be used for His glory through suffering?
- Have you asked Him for the opportunity to suffer for His sake if that would glorify Him the most in your life?

12. Direct all credit given to us on to God.

> *But by the grace of God I am what I am, and His grace toward me did not prove vain; but I labored even more than all of them, yet not I, but the grace of God with me.*
> *1 Corinthians 15:10, emphasis added*

> *For through the grace given to me I say to every man among you not to think more highly of himself than he ought to think; but to think so as to have sound judgment, as God has allotted to each a measure of faith.*
> *Romans 12:3, emphasis added*

> *Not to us, O LORD, not to us, but to Your name give glory. Because of Your lovingkindness, because of Your truth.*
> *Psalm 115:1*

Questions:

- When someone praises you or thanks you do you think, "Lord, this is really a sacrifice of praise to you. You deserve all the credit and glory for this gift or talent you gave me"?

- Do you realize that apart from God, you can do nothing? That any ability you have to work and earn money, to think and plan, to help others, or live another day is a grace gift from God?

13. Pray.

> *And when you pray do not use meaningless repetition as the Gentiles do, for they suppose that they will be heard for their many words. Therefore do not be like them; for your Father knows what you need before you ask Him. Pray, then, in this way...*   *Matthew 6:7-8*

> *And this I pray, that your love may abound still more and more in real knowledge and all discernment, so that you may approve the things that are excellent, in order to be sincere and blameless until the day of Christ; having been filled with the fruit of righteousness which comes through Jesus Christ, to the glory and praise of God.*
> *Philippians 1:9-11*

Whatever you ask in My name, that will I do, so that the Father may be glorified in the Son.　　　　*John 14:13*

Questions:

- Do you realize that the basis for all petitions to God is His glory?

- Do you pray for God's will to be done in your life and the lives of others?

- Do you pray that God will be glorified by your every thought, word, and deed?

What is your view of God? Is it high (like Daniel's view) or low (like psychologized and religious man's views)? Are you truly bowing before Him in every area of your life or are you using Him to meet your needs? God is holy and awesome. We should approach Him with great care and respect. We should see that we are here to serve Him; He is not here to serve us.

Consider the following contrast:

MAN-CENTERED VIEW OF GOD	GOD-CENTERED VIEW OF GOD
You take the initiative in your salvation.	God takes the initiative in your salvation.　　　Ephesians 1:3-4
God is here to meet your identity needs.	God is here to glorify Himself.　　　Isaiah 42:8
God needs you.	God needs no one but chose to create us for His own glorious purpose.　　　Ephesians 1:14
You grow as a Christian by getting in touch with your deepest emotional pain and then realizing that your identity is in Christ.	You grow as a Christian by turning from your sinful self-focus and by obeying God's Word whether you feel like it or not.　　　Ephesians 4:22-24
You seek the accolades of others.	You seek the glory of God　　　1 Corinthians 10:31
You seek love and approval and esteem.	You repent of your self-focus and seek to give love to others and to God.　　　Matthew 22:39

Conclusion

Daniel saw God as lofty and exalted. He bowed low before Him and prayed often to *God Most High*. Daniel served God in many ways that showed his sincere concern for God's glory and worth. Daniel was a humble man.

Religious man, on the other hand, sees God somewhat as a puppet on a string to do his bidding. He thinks that his good thoughts or actions obligate God to save him. Religious man serves God but for the wrong reasons. He is proud.

Psychologized man tries to use God to satisfy his longings to feel worthy or significant. He is man-centered and seeks his own esteem rather than God's glory. Psychologized man will never be satisfied. He is selfish.

Of the three men, Daniel is the only one who held a high and proper view of God. Which of the three are you most like - Daniel, religious man, or psychologized man? If the answer is anything other than "I am like Daniel," your thoughts are conformed to the world's way of thinking. I would urge you to prayerfully consider what you have learned from these first five chapters and begin, today, to give God the glory that He alone is due!

In Part I of this book, we have seen Daniel's view of God Most High, Religious Man, Psychologized Man, what our High and Holy God is really like, and finally His High and Holy standards. As we move forward to explain other aspects of a transformed mind such as "Attitudes and Scripture" and "Attitudes of Heart," keep in mind that right beliefs about God are fundamental and critical to the *Attitudes of a Transformed Heart*.

There is a hymn by Avis Christiansen that I love entitled "Only One Life."[34] Think about the words and think about your life...

> Only one life to offer - Jesus, my Lord and King;
> Only one tongue to praise Thee and of Thy mercy sing (forever);
> Only one heart's devotion - Savior, O may it be
> Consecrated alone to Thy matchless glory, yielded fully to Thee.
>
> Only this hour is mine Lord - may it be used for Thee;
> May every passing moment count for eternity (my Savior);
> Souls all about are dying, dying in sin and shame;
> Help me bring them the message of Calv'ry's redemption in thy glorious name.
>
> Only one life to offer - take it, dear Lord, I pray;
> Nothing from Thee withholding, Thy will I now obey (my Jesus);
> Thou who hast freely given Thine all in all for me,
> Claim this life for Thine own to be used, my
> Savior, ev'ry moment for thee.

What is your prayer?

∞

Chapter 5

Study Questions

In this chapter there are thirteen biblical ways to glorify God. Under each way to glorify God there are several questions. Read back over all the Scriptures and questions. Write down in your own words what you know you need to confess, for which you need to ask God's help. For each one that needs improvement, give several practical examples of how to do so.

Example:

Principle: Aim my life exclusively at God's glory.

Because I serve others and am in the background, I sometimes struggle with wanting the attention that others are receiving. Instead I need to ask God to continue to use me for His glory whether anyone at church recognizes my work or not.

Many times my secret thoughts do not glorify God. I need to confess those when they occur and think God-glorifying thoughts instead. For example, instead of thinking, "I hate my house. Why doesn't God give me a better house?" I should think, "Lord *thank You* for this house. Help me to be content and may *You* be glorified in my thoughts whether I ever have a different house or not."

Part Two

Attitudes and Scripture

"How sweet are Your words to my taste!
Yes, sweeter than honey to my mouth!
From Your precepts I get understanding;
Therefore I hate every false way."
Psalm 119:103-104

Chapter 6

Doctrine

Before I became a Christian, I would frequently become enamoured with something such as a new job or new degree and pursue it with great enthusiasm. At least, I would pursue it for a while until the novelty wore off, and then I would be on to the next great adventure. This pattern was so obvious in my life that when I became a Christian, my Mother told me, "You'll pursue Christianity for a while and then move on to something else." I knew that knowing the Lord was different, but I also knew that she had a good point. So I said, "I can understand why you think this is another phase in my life because of all I have done in the past." Later, as I thought about my tendency to jump from one project to another, I was grieved to think that my newfound passion for the Lord might likewise fade into oblivion. Knowing my weakness, I turned to God for help and I prayed, "Lord, my prayer is that You will give me such a great love for Your Word that no matter how much I learn, I will never be satisfied. I will always want to know more." That prayer was prayed over twenty years ago, and God has been faithful to grant me my desire. My initial excitement about the Lord has passed, but never has my love and longing to know more of Him through His Word.

If you want to know more about God and want to please Him, then you have to study His Word. There is no short cut or substitute. It is one of the primary means that God uses to renew our minds. The Scriptures were given **"for our instruction"** (Romans 15:4). Part of that **"instruction"** is for us to be able to discern unbiblical thoughts and the world's way of thinking. Thus, the Scriptures are one means of God's grace to us in the process of growing as Christians into Christlikeness. We cannot rightly apply to our life something we do not know or something we have misinterpreted. The Scriptures could be compared to a recipe. If you misread the recipe, no one will be able to eat your cake. Like reading the recipe correctly so that your cake will be good, you must study the Scriptures because they are a direct and critical link to being **"trans-**

formed by the renewing of your mind..." (Romans 12:2).

When you study the Bible, you are studying Bible doctrine. Bible doctrine is simply what the Bible teaches about a particular subject. It is how the teachings of the Bible fit together. For example, the doctrine of the Trinity is what the Bible teaches about God the Father, Son, and Holy Spirit. Another example is the doctrine of sin. A proper understanding of sin can only be found from considering the passages throughout Scripture that teach us about sin and transgressing against God's Law. We have to consider the whole counsel of God which is His Word and rightly interpret it in the context in which it was written. The Scriptures are literally **"...inspired by God and profitable for...teaching [doctrine]..."** (2 Timothy 3:16, explanation added).

Certainly there are many different Bible teachings that directly affect our thinking. However, for the purpose of this book, in this section we will consider three of them - (1) Doctrine, (2) Practical Application of Doctrine: Guidance from God, and (3) Practical Application of Doctrine: Worship. Let's begin with doctrine.

The Importance of Doctrine

Why is knowing and applying Bible doctrine so important? What does doctrine have to do with a transformed heart? First of all, you must study doctrine so that you will not be deceived and will be mature.

> *And He [Christ] gave some as apostles, and some as prophets, and some as evangelists, and some as pastors and teachers, for the equipping of the saints for the work of service, to the building up of the body of Christ; <u>until we all attain to the unity of the faith, and of the knowledge of the Son of God, to a mature man, to the measure of the stature which belongs to the fullness of Christ</u>...*
> *Ephesians 4:11-13, emphasis added*

God has gifted each believer with spiritual gifts so they will be equipped to serve in the church. As each member of the body of Christ uses his/her gifts, some of them will teach Bible doctrine helping others to become more discerning, less easily deceived by false doctrine, and more mature in the Lord.

> *As a result, <u>we are no longer to be children</u>, tossed here and there by waves and carried about by every wind of doctrine, by the trickery of men, <u>by craftiness in deceitful scheming</u>; but speaking the truth in love, <u>we are to grow</u>*

> *up in all aspects into Him who is the head, even Christ,*
> *from whom the whole body, being fitted and held together*
> *by what every joint supplies, according to the proper*
> *working of each individual part, causes the growth of the*
> *body for the building up of itself in love.*
> Ephesians 4:14-16, emphasis added

In addition to *not* being deceived and *to* being mature, you must also study what is written in the Scriptures (Bible doctrine) so that you can be personally pure.

> *How can a young man keep his way pure?*
> *By keeping it according to Your word.*   Psalm 119:9

Often you hear people say, "She has head knowledge, but not heart knowledge." I assume they mean that she has some knowledge about the Scriptures, but does not apply it to her life or have affections for the Lord. Some people, on the other hand, seek to gain a "heart knowledge" solely through emotional experiences while they know nothing about the Bible. The solution, however, is to study the doctrine *and* to apply what you have learned (Ezra 7:10). This will allow one's heart knowledge to flow out of one's head knowledge. No one can become more personally pure without first studying the Scriptures.

When I was studying to become a nurse, we learned in the classroom how to perform nursing procedures on patients. Only then did we go to the hospital and begin to practice those procedures – first on mannequins, sometimes on each other, and ultimately on real live patients. At first we were all awkward, clumsy, slow, and unsure. It was only after much experience that we became competent and highly skilled. As a student nurse has to learn the theory of nursing *before* she can learn to apply it, a Christian *has* to learn Bible doctrine before she can apply it to her life.

It is true what my friend, Howard Dial, pastor of Berachah Bible Church in Fayetteville, Georgia, used to tell us, "There is no substitute for verse-by-verse exposition of the Word of God." If you want to be God-like and not think of Him as the world does, you must study God. The only place we can study God is in His Word, the Bible. This truth is why it is so critically important to place yourself in a church that takes study of the Scriptures seriously. Only then will you be able to **"grow in the grace and knowledge of our Lord and Savior Jesus Christ"** (2 Peter 3:18). Let's now consider seven biblical principles concerning the importance of Bible doctrine.

Biblical Principles on Doctrine

1. We are to be mature in our understanding of Bible doctrine so that we will not be deceived.

   As a result, we are no longer to be children, tossed here and there by waves, and carried about by every wind of doctrine...   Ephesians 4:14

2. A person who advocates unbiblical doctrine has a corrupt mind and has been deprived of the truth.

   If anyone advocates a different doctrine [other than what the Bible teaches], and does not agree with sound words, those of our Lord Jesus Christ, and with the doctrine conforming to godliness, he is conceited and understands nothing; but he has a morbid interest in controversial questions and disputes about words, out of which arise envy, strife, abusive language, evil suspicions, and constant friction between men of depraved mind and deprived of the truth, who suppose that godliness is a means of gain...   1 Timothy 6:3-5, explanation added

3. Unsaved people grow more and more intolerant of sound doctrine.

   For the time will come when they will not endure sound doctrine; but wanting to have their ears tickled, they will accumulate for themselves teachers in accordance to their own desires; and will turn away their ears from the truth, and will turn aside to myths.   2 Timothy 4:3-4

4. The elders are to hold fast to sound doctrine, be able to teach sound doctrine, and to refute those who contradict it.

   For the overseer [pastor or elder] must be ... holding fast the faithful word which is in accordance with the teaching, that he may be able both to exhort in sound doctrine and to refute those who contradict.
   Titus 1:7-9, explanation added

5. Religious people who teach man's doctrines are worshiping Christ in vain.

    > *[Jesus said to the Pharisees], "You hypocrites, rightly did Isaiah prophesy of you, saying, 'This people honors Me with their lips, but their heart is far away from Me. But in vain do they worship Me, teaching as their doctrines the precepts of men.'"*
    > *Matthew 15:7-9, explanation added*

6. Pastors are to teach sound doctrine to the older women so the older women can teach and encourage the younger women in order that the Word of God will not be dishonored.

    > *But as for you [Titus], speak the things which are fitting for sound doctrine...Older women likewise are to be ... teaching what is good, that they may encourage the younger women ... that the word of God may not be dishonored.*
    > *Titus 2:1,3-5, explanation added*

7. The Scripture and its teachings are referred to in a variety of ways. In Psalm 119 for example, it is called God's Law, His testimony, God's precepts, His ways, His statutes, His commandments, His judgments, His rules on life, God's Word, God's sayings, and our path.

    > *How blessed are those who observe His testimonies...*
    > *Psalm 119:2a*

    > *Oh that my ways may be established to keep Thy statutes!*
    > *Psalm 119:5*

    > *Make me walk in the path of Thy commandments...*
    > *Psalm 119:35a*

    > *It is good for me that I was afflicted, that I may learn Thy statutes.*
    > *Psalm 119:71*

    > *From Thy precepts I get understanding...Psalm 119:104a*

The Bible contains many commands, examples, and promises that tell us exactly *why* we should push forward in the study of the Scriptures. Let's look at why it is so important that we study Bible doctrine.

Why Study Bible Doctrine?

1. Bible doctrine is a major priority of the New Testament church.

    And they [the new believers] were continually devoting themselves to the apostles' teaching [doctrine] and to fellowship, to the breaking of bread and to prayer.
    Acts 2:42, explanation added

2. Bible doctrine is a vital item in the Christian's armor.

    Stand firm therefore, having girded your loins with truth...and take ... the sword of the Spirit, which is the word of God.   *Ephesians 6:14, 17 emphasis added*

3. We must be *increasing* in Bible knowledge if we are never to stumble.

    Now for this very reason also, applying all diligence, in your faith supply moral excellence, and in your moral excellence, knowledge ...For if these qualities are yours and are increasing, they render you neither useless nor unfruitful in the true knowledge of our Lord Jesus Christ...Therefore, brethren, be all the more diligent to make certain about His calling and choosing you; for as long as you practice these things, you will never stumble...
    2 Peter 1:5-10, emphasis added

4. Understanding and living Bible doctrine is the *command* of God.

    But He [Jesus] answered and said, "It is written, Man shall not live on bread alone, but on every word that proceeds out of the mouth of God."
    Matthew 4:4, explanation added

5. Bible doctrine leads to glorifying God's holy name.

    I will bow down toward Thy holy temple, and give thanks to Thy name for Thy lovingkindness and Thy truth; for Thou hast magnified Thy word according to all Thy name.
    Psalm 138:2

6. Bible doctrine leads to gratitude to the Lord.

    Let the word of Christ richly dwell within you, with all wisdom teaching and admonishing one another with psalms and hymns and spiritual songs, singing with thankfulness in your hearts to God.   Colossians 3:16

7. Bible doctrine leads to outstanding wisdom.

    Thy commandments make me wiser than my enemies, for they are ever mine. I have more insight than all my teachers, for Thy testimonies are my meditation. I understand more than the aged, because I have observed Thy precepts.
    Psalm 119:98-100

8. Bible doctrine is more valuable than daily food.

    I have not departed from the command of His lips; I have treasured the words of His mouth more than my necessary food.   Job 23:12

9. We must have Bible doctrine to grow spiritually. We should long for it.

    ...like newborn babes, long for the pure milk of the word, that by it you may grow in respect to salvation, if you have tasted the kindness of the Lord.   1 Peter 2:2-3

10. If we remain and persevere in Jesus' teachings, we will bear fruit.

    [Jesus said,] "If you abide in Me, and My words abide in you, ask whatever you wish, and it shall be done for you. By this is My Father glorified, that you bear much fruit, and so prove to be My disciples."   John 15:7-8

11.   We must have the Word abiding in us to have victory over Satan.

> *I have written to you, fathers, because you know Him who has been from the beginning. I have written to you, young men, because you are strong, and the word of God abides in you, and you have overcome the evil one.*
> **1 John 2:14**

12.   Bible doctrine is the only way to true freedom.

> *Jesus therefore was saying to those Jews who had believed Him, "If you abide in My word, then you are truly disciples of Mine; and you shall know the truth, and the truth shall make you free."*   **John 8:31-32**

13.   We must have doctrine to be adequately equipped for ministry.

> *All Scripture is inspired by God and profitable for teaching [doctrine], for reproof, for correction, for training in righteousness; that the man of God may be adequate, equipped for every good work.*
> **2 Timothy 3:16-17, explanation added**

14.   Bible doctrine is a means of saving faith.

> *So faith comes from hearing ... the word of Christ.*
> **Romans 10:17**

15.   Bible doctrine will comfort us in affliction.

> *This is my comfort in my affliction, that Thy word has revived me.*   **Psalm 119:50**

Studying Bible doctrine is vital for every Christian. We have just seen fifteen reasons *why* we should study the Bible. Now let's turn our attention to the practical relationship between understanding Bible doctrine and the renewing of the mind.

The Practical Relationship between Bible Doctrine and the Renewing of the Mind

You may have heard the example of the bank employees or federal agents who are trained to recognize counterfeit dollar bills. Interestingly they do not spend their time studying the counterfeit bills, but rather the real money. They know what real money feels like and looks like. They also know all the tiny little details of the words and symbols on the bills, as well as the color of the print. So when the counterfeit comes along, no matter how good the copy is, it is obviously a fake to them. In the same way, if you are going to know what the Lord Jesus Christ is like and how you are to think and what your attitudes are to be, you must study the Scriptures. Only then will you have the discernment to recognize counterfeit teachings about Christ.

The Scriptures tell us what we need to know about the Lord Jesus in order to be like Him. He is the only example we have of someone who lived a perfectly sinless life (2 Corinthians 5:21). He is the only one who perfectly obeyed the Father even to the **"point of death"** (Philippians 2:8). The Lord Jesus understands our weaknesses and so He helps us (Hebrews 2:18). We are to be like Him not only in outward actions but also in our attitudes (Philippians 2:5). We are to **"fix our eyes on Jesus"** and since we cannot see Him physically right now, we must see what He is like through the Scriptures (Hebrews 12:2). The more we study the Scriptures, the more we will know Him.

In addition to pursuing Bible doctrine (and thus learning what the Lord Jesus is like) so that you may think biblically, you should understand that Scripture can help you resist temptation. Of course, the supreme example of someone using Scripture in a way to resist temptation is the Lord Jesus Christ when He was tempted by Satan.

> *Then Jesus was led up by the Spirit into the wilderness to be tempted by the devil. And after He had fasted forty days and forty nights, He then became hungry. And the tempter came and said to Him, "If you are the Son of God, command that these stones become bread." But He answered and said, "It is written, 'Man shall not live on bread alone, but on every word that proceeds out of the mouth of God.'" Then the devil took Him into the holy city and had Him stand on the pinnacle of the temple, and said to Him, "If you are the Son of God, throw Yourself down; for it is written, 'He will command His angels concerning you'; and 'On their hands they will bear You*

*up, so that You will not strike Your foot against a stone.'"
Jesus said to him, "On the other hand, it is written, 'You
shall not put the Lord your God to the test.'" Again, the
devil took Him to a very high mountain and showed Him
all the kingdoms of the world and their glory; and he said
to Him, "All these things I will give you, if you fall down
and worship me." Then Jesus said to him, "Begone, Satan! For it is written, 'You shall worship the LORD your
God, and serve Him only.'"* **Matthew 4:1-10**

Scripture is powerful. It is powerful not in some magical, wave a wand, hocus-pocus, utter a few Scriptures and sprinkle magic dust sort of way, but powerful through the supernatural grace of God to help us resist temptation. Did you notice that in the previously quoted passage, Satan also used Scripture verses to prove his point? He misused and twisted them for his own personal ends. We must be careful to follow Christ's example rather than Satan's. The example the Lord Jesus gives us is to learn God's Word in its *context* so that we may rightly use the Scriptures to resist temptation.

So far we have seen the practical relationship between Bible doctrine and a renewed mind in two ways: first, we must study God's Word to learn what the Lord Jesus Christ is like so that we may be like Him, and second, we should learn God's Word to help us resist temptation. It goes without saying that in order to accomplish these goals, we need to study the Scriptures personally.

Conclusion

The original readers of the letter entitled *Hebrews* were acting like babies when it came to their ability to "digest" and benefit from the Word of God. By the time *Hebrews* was written, the readers should have understood basic Bible doctrine and become teachers of others. Instead they were like babies who should have already been on solid food but were still carrying around their cups of milk.

> **For though by this time you ought to be teachers; you have need again for someone to teach you the elementary principles of the oracles of God, and you have come to need milk and not solid food. For everyone who partakes only of milk is not accustomed to the word of righteousness, for he is a babe. But solid food is for the mature, who because of practice have their senses trained to discern good and evil.   Hebrews 5:12-14**

Thus we too must have solid food from God's Word. We like them must be fed from pastors and teachers who are men of integrity who study the Scriptures and in turn feed their flocks. We must also study the Scriptures for ourselves being like the Bereans who **"received the word with great eagerness, examining the Scriptures daily to see whether these things were so"** (Acts 17:11; see also 2 Timothy 2:15).

Scripture study is a lost art for many Christians. Often, they are busy with programs and church projects that, frankly, keep them away from God and His Word. How tragic and unnecessary that one could spend an entire life having been the hardest and most dependable worker in the church and yet not have honored the Lord through personal study of His Word. Often pastors do not study as they should and, as a result, they do not teach their people how to study. Shallow sermons lead to shallow, immature Christians. Shallow, immature Christians do not know how to teach the children Bible doctrine. Often they fill up all of what could be teaching time with skits and programs. Even though it is not wrong, for example, to teach the children creatively about missionaries by dressing up like people in Zaire or Japan, it *is* wrong to replace teaching them sound doctrine with such programs. I am sure that Satan would much rather have us spend all our time with the children of the church preparing a typical meal that a foreign missionary might eat rather than spending most of our time teaching the children Bible doctrine with a few minutes of practical and concrete examples also in the lesson.

Because Bible doctrine is so critical to holy living, our use of time should reflect its importance (see 1 Timothy 4:7-8). We should be organized and include time in our day to read, study, and meditate on the Word of God. It should be a priority, not an afterthought at the end of the day. If you do not have time, ask yourself these questions: Do I watch television? How much time do I spend on the telephone talking to my friends? How much time do I spend shopping? Exercising? Can't I cut out some of these (and other) less important activities to give myself the time I need to read God's Word? You see, each of us is going to do what is really important to us.

How God-honoring your thoughts are and how much like Him you become depends on how much sound Bible doctrine you know and apply to your life. Growth begins with knowledge of who God is, knowledge of how God thinks, and knowledge of what God wants you to do. How serious are you about wanting to honor God and not be conformed to thinking and acting like this world?

> *Your Word I have treasured in my heart,*
> *That I may not sin against You.*
> **Psalm 119:11**

Chapter 5

Study Questions

1. What is Bible doctrine?

2. Give two examples of Bible doctrine.

3. According to Ephesians 4:11-16, what do spiritual gifts have to do with Bible doctrine?

4. Why is "head knowledge" important?

5. Match the following:

Religious people who teach men's doctrines are not really worshiping Christ.	1 Timothy 6:3-5
The pastor is to refute those who oppose sound doctrine.	Titus 2:1,3-5
Unsaved people are intolerant of sound doctrine.	2 Timothy 4:3-4
There is a link between a corrupt mind and unbiblical doctrine.	Matthew 15:7-9
The older women are to teach the younger women sound doctrine.	Titus 1:7-9

6. Write down how many reasons you can remember (without looking) from the list "Why study Bible Doctrine?" After you have written down what you can remember, review the fifteen reasons on pages 92-94.

7. What is the connection between pursuing Bible doctrine and resisting temptation?

8. Why is it so important that you be taught Bible doctrine by your pastor and that you also study on your own? See Hebrews 5:12-14

9. How much time do you plan in your day to read, study, and meditate on God's Word?

10. How much time *should* you plan in your day to read, study, and meditate on God's Word?

11. How could you rearrange your priorities to include the study of Scripture?

Chapter 7

Practical Application of Doctrine: Guidance

I can see and hear myself from years past saying, "I have peace about my decision;" or "I feel led;" or "There is no doubt in my mind that God wants me to ..." Now I hear myself saying, "This is an area in which I have freedom;" or "What do the Scriptures say?" or "Lord, as best I can determine You want me to do ...;" and lastly, "If You have a different plan I know You'll make it clear." I have heard others say, "The Lord told me to ..." or "I saw a vision," or "The Lord spoke to me last night in a dream." There are almost as many views of guidance from God as there are Christians! The reason I chose this particular topic in Part II - Attitudes and Scripture is because the issue of guidance directly relates to knowing the will of God. The will of God is affirmed in our lives as good and acceptable and perfect to the degree that we have been *"transformed by the renewing of [our] mind[s]..."* (Romans 12:2, adaptation added).

If your view of how God guides you is not true to the Scriptures then you could wrongly discern His will and not even know it. You also could be giving out very definite advice and directing other people's lives in an unbiblical way that God never intended. For a Christian who desires more than anything to please the Lord, this is a very disturbing thought. Is God speaking directly to us through a still, small voice? Does He lead us through our emotions and feelings such as "I feel led" or "I have peace"? Is He guiding us at all or simply leaving us to fend for ourselves? Your answers to these questions (your view of how God is guiding you) will directly affect your walk with Him and thus your thoughts and attitudes. I would ask you to prayerfully consider the material in this chapter because if we are going to not be like the world then it follows that we are **"not [to] be foolish but *understand* what the will of the Lord is"** (Ephesians 5:17, emphasis and adaptation added).

Christians do want to understand God's will. They want to know with certainty how God is guiding them so they may know His will. In the South we have an expression that confirms whether something is true or not. Whereas others might say, "Really?" or "Is that so?", Southerners might say, "For sure?" So, if you want to know *for sure* how God guides you, you must go to the Scriptures (God's *for sure* Word) to find answers. After all, His Word is perfect, sure, right, pure, clean, and true.

> *The law of the LORD is <u>perfect</u>, restoring the soul; the testimony of the LORD is <u>sure</u>, making wise the simple. The precepts of the LORD are <u>right</u>, rejoicing the heart; the commandment of the LORD is <u>pure</u>, enlightening the eyes. The fear of the LORD is <u>clean</u>, enduring forever; the judgments of the LORD are <u>true</u>; they are righteous altogether.* **Psalm 19:7-8, emphasis added**

If we are truly going to *understand* how God guides us to know His will for us, then we need to begin with what we can know *for sure*. After that we will consider what we don't know for sure and how what we don't know could pull us off track and out of God's will. Let's begin, however, with what we know – *for sure*.

What We Can Know For Sure

One thing that we know *for sure* is that God is sovereign. As we mentioned earlier in this book, God is the Ruler of His universe that He created. He is constantly, actively, providentially working in His creation to accomplish His will and He rules whether His creatures like it or not. God's sovereignty has a direct bearing on how He guides us. It is through His ruling grace over us that His will often is revealed to us. For example, missionaries may go to countries where the government officials are not overly fond of Christians. But because God channels the hearts of kings (Proverbs 21:1), the missionaries are permitted to come into their country anyway. So God is sovereignly permitting or limiting missionaries to go into certain countries.

The second thing we can know *for sure* how God guides us is His will for us as it is revealed in Scripture. From the Scriptures, we clearly know some parts of God's will — the Ten Commandments, for example. There is no dispute about the following sample of mandates from God:

> **You shall have no other gods before Me.**
> **You shall not murder.**
> **You shall not commit adultery.**
> **You shall not steal. (Exodus 20:3,13-15)**

Let's begin by considering what we know from Scripture about God's will that *is* revealed to us in a clear, straightforward manner.

What We Know From Scripture About God's Will[35]

1. It is God's will that you be Spirit-filled.

    > *So then do not be foolish, but understand what the will of the Lord is. And do not get drunk with wine, for that is dissipation [utter ruin], but be filled with the Spirit...*
    > *Ephesians 5:17-18, explanation and emphasis added*

    The Spirit-filled life is living every moment being controlled by the Holy Spirit. This means you must be saturated with the things of Christ and His Word (Colossians 3:16). For example, one specific way the Spirit-filled life is manifested is through **"always giving thanks for all things in the name of our Lord Jesus Christ to God, even the Father..."** (Ephesians 5:20).

2. It is God's will that you be morally pure.

    > *For this is the will of God, your sanctification; that is, that you abstain from sexual immorality...*
    > *1 Thessalonians 4:3*

    What we do with our bodies either glorifies God or it does not. What we allow to cross our minds either glorifies God or it does not. There is no question that our bodies are to be enjoyed sexually within marriage in a way that pleases God instead of offends Him. Christians must remember that they have been **"bought with a price [the blood of the Lord Jesus Christ]: therefore [they are to] glorify God in [their] body"** (1 Corinthians 6:20, adaptation added).

3. It is God's will that you suffer as a Christian.

    > *If you are reviled for the name of Christ, you are blessed, because the Spirit of glory and of God rests on you. By no means let any of you suffer as a murderer, or thief, or evildoer, or a troublesome meddler; but if anyone suffers as a Christian, let him not feel ashamed but in that name let him glorify God ... Therefore, let those also who suffer according to the will of God entrust their souls to a faithful Creator in doing what is right.*
    > *1 Peter 4:14-16,19*

Because the darkness hates the light, unbelievers persecute believers for their beliefs and faith. They slander those who love the Lord and cut off life-long friendships. Some Christians suffer imprisonment and even death for their faith. It should come as no surprise that those who **"desire to live godly in Christ Jesus will be persecuted"** (2 Timothy 3:12; see also Philippians 1:29). Somehow God uses the persecution of Christians to glorify Himself and to help mold them into greater Christlikeness. It is God's will that we suffer for righteousness sake.

4. It is God's will that you be submissive.

> *Submit yourselves for the Lord's sake to every human in-stitution, whether to a king as the one in authority, or to governors as sent by him for the punishment of evildoers and the praise of those who do right. For such is the will of God that by doing right you may silence the ignorance of foolish men.*   *1 Peter 2:13-15*

Certainly Christians are to obey their government unless their government requires them to sin. They are also to obey others God has placed in authority over them. Some examples include a husband in authority over his wife or a parent in authority over a child. We are to obey unless our authority asks us to sin. Then we must obey God who is always the highest authority (Acts 5:29). God's will is partially revealed in Scripture through clear and understandable passages – it is God's will that you be Spirit-filled, morally pure, submissive, and suffering. These are examples of things we can know *for sure*.

What We Know from Providence about God's Will

In addition to what we know from Scripture about God's will, we also know that God is guiding us through His providential care. "Providence concerns God's creation, from the moment of the first creation to all the future into eternity. Providence is God's activity through His unlimited power and knowledge to fulfill His purpose for the whole creation, including man."[36] How God is providentially working in and guiding His creation is a mystery that we cannot fully comprehend. We can, however, sometimes realize God's working in our life but then usually only in retrospect. Until then, it is a secret known only to God.

> *The mind of man plans his way, but the LORD directs his steps.*   *Proverbs 16:9*

The secret things belong to the LORD our God, but the things revealed belong to us and to our sons forever, that we may observe all the words of this law.
                                                                    Deuteronomy 29:29

One example of God working providentially is how He **"causes all things [both good and bad] to work together for good for those who love God"** (Romans 8:28, explanation added). God wonderfully works in our lives through His perfect knowledge of and sovereign control over our circumstances to bring blessings and testings our way. Nothing happens to us by chance or fate, not even the tiniest little detail of our circumstances. He somehow takes all that happens to us and works it in our lives to make us more like the Lord Jesus Christ. Even though it is a secret, we do know that God is providentially, supernaturally arranging our circumstances and thus is guiding our way. When you consider God's directives to us through Scripture combined together with His providential care over us, you know what we may know *for sure* about God's guidance.

Now let's turn to a different issue – what we cannot know for sure.

What We Cannot Know for Sure[37]

What we cannot know *for sure* are some of the methods of guidance that many, if not most, Christians depend upon. As you read through the following list, please consider what we have seen that we can know and compare to the following.

1. Let your conscience be your guide.

> *I thank God, whom I serve with a clear conscience the way my forefathers did, as I constantly remember you in my prayers night and day...*   *2 Timothy 1:3*

In the previous passage the Apostle Paul is not writing about how God was guiding him. Rather he is simply stating the fact that as of that particular moment, his conscience was clear. Unfortunately, many Christians refer to verses such as this one and understand them to mean God's guidance of them is known through having a clear conscience. Certainly it is possible for God to convict us and cause us to feel guilty about sin, but whether we feel guilty or not is not a good way to ascertain God's guidance because our consciences may have been wrongly influenced. To the degree that we have studied God's Word in context and made appropriate applications, our conscience will have been rightly influenced. Only then will we be able to discern between **"good and evil"** (Hebrews 5:14). I have heard many women say to me, "God understands what I am about to do. I just feel that it is right." Sometimes what they felt was right was obviously wrong! So relying on your conscience to guide you would have to be in the category of what we *cannot* know *for sure*.

2. "I feel led."

> *However, you are not in the flesh but in the Spirit, if indeed the Spirit of God dwells in you ...So then, brethren, we are under obligation, not to the flesh, to live according to the flesh — for if you are living according to the flesh, you must die; but if by the Spirit you are putting to death the deeds of the body, you will live. For all who are being led by the Spirit of God, these are sons of God.*
>
> *Romans 8:9-14*

All Christians have Christ indwelling them and they can look forward to the resurrection of their physical bodies that someday will be pure, holy, and sinless. Meanwhile, Christians are under obligation to put to death the deeds of the flesh. Obedient Christians who put to death the deeds of the flesh *are* those being led by the Holy Spirit. This is a fact, not a feeling. When we assume that a desire or a feeling ("impressions," "checks in my spirit," "a still small voice," "having peace or not having peace") is the Spirit of God leading us, we open ourselves and others up to confusion and error. An obvious example of God not leading would be the woman who felt it right to consult a fortuneteller. A less obvious example would be a mother who feels a check in her spirit concerning the young man her daughter wishes to marry. Without objective criteria to back up her concern, she is in danger of misleading her daughter. Whenever our feelings become the standard instead of God's Word, we move dangerously away from what we know *for sure*.

3. I must "let go and let God."

> *Though youths grow weary and tired and vigorous young men stumble badly, yet those <u>who wait on the LORD will gain new strength</u>; they shall mount up with wings like eagles, they shall run and not be tired, they shall walk and not become weary.*
>
> *Isaiah 40:31, emphasis added*

What a soul-stirring verse! It is one that is commonly seen on plaques and pictures in Christian bookstores, but it is one that is commonly pulled out of its context. Certainly all Scripture is profitable to teach us, but not all Scripture is written directly to us. This passage in Isaiah chapter forty is written directly to the Jews in King Hezekiah's day to warn them of judgment to come. It was written to them for comfort, and for us to know more about the character of God and how He is just, but also merciful. It is not a verse on how God guides us. Trying to "let go and let God" is a rather vague mysterious concept that is unclear and dependant on individual interpretation. Rather than teaching us to sit back and "let God," the Scriptures teach us to enjoy the freedom we have in Christ, but to not use this freedom as an excuse for sin or license to sin (Romans 6:15-18). The Scriptures also teach that instead of sitting back and "letting God," we are responsible to work at mortifying the flesh and putting on virtue. For example, we are to put off anger and put on a kind and tender heart (Ephesians 4:31-32). Some might think that we are taking away from God's glory if we work at putting on Christian virtues. On the contrary, if one seeks to become more godly because one loves the Lord and desires to please Him, they *are* giving God the glory and credit because they cannot possibly honor Him without the empowering grace of the Holy Spirit to enable them. Instead of relying on some sort of personal experience ("*I* must let go") to know God's guidance, we are to stick with what we know *for sure*. What we know *for sure* is the Scriptures understood in their context.

4.   Three others agree with me so it must be God's will.

> *Truly I [the Lord Jesus] say to you, whatever you bind on earth shall have been bound in heaven; and whatever you loose on earth shall have been loosed in heaven. Again I say to you, that if two of you agree on earth about anything that they may ask, it shall be done for them by My Father who is in heaven.*
> *Matthew 18:18-19, explanation added*

Next to **"judge not that ye be not judged"** in Matthew chapter seven, this Matthew chapter eighteen verse **"if two of you agree on earth"** must be the verse most often taken out of its intended context. The context is clearly and directly the subject of church discipline. In Matthew 18:15-17, the Lord explains what to do if a Christian brother or sister is sinning. First, go to them privately. If they don't repent, take two or more witnesses with you and confront them again. Then if they still refuse to repent, their lack of repentance is to be told to the church. If they still refuse to repent even after the church members have exhorted them, then they are to be considered as an unbeliever. Church discipline is what this passage on **"two or more agreeing"** is about, not how God guides us.

5.   God has given me an open door so it must be His will.

> *[The Apostle Paul speaking:] Now when I came to Troas for the gospel of Christ and when a door was opened for me in the Lord, I had no rest for my spirit, not finding Titus my brother; but taking my leave of them, I went on to Macedonia.*
>
> *2 Corinthians 2:12-13, explanation added*

"A door was opened for me in the Lord" was an opportunity for evangelism for Paul. This open door is a figure of speech, not a literal door. In other words, an "open door for the gospel" was God preparing people's hearts to believe and providing Paul the opportunity to give them the gospel. It is not a verse on guidance. Open or closed doors in reference to guidance has become a Christian cliché that is overused and misused. The most we should say about any apparently God-given opportunity is, "As well as I can know *for sure* from Scripture, this opportunity is one that I have freedom from God to pursue. If the Lord has other plans, I trust Him to make it obvious."

Conclusion

When we consider how God guides us, we also must remember that our hearts deceive us. We are capable of believing and feeling that God is guiding us when really our consciences may have been taught error instead of truth. What we *feel* we desire to do is simply that – our feeling. It is possible to have a feeling and think God is leading us when what we really have is an idol perhaps of controlling others or fear of man. The only *for sure* way to know God's will is to go to the Scriptures.

From the Scriptures we know that God is sovereign and rules the universe He created. He is actively working in His creation to accomplish His will. We know that it is God's will that we be saturated with the things of Christ and His Word and live our lives aware of being in the presence of Jesus Christ. We are also to be morally pure and submissive to those in authority over us and, at times, it is God's will that we suffer for Jesus' sake as Christians. These are what we can know about God's will for us.

Being guided by God is not something over which we need to agonize. Instead it should be a joy knowing that God is working in our lives and guiding us clearly through His Word and secretly through His providential care.

It is a mark of maturity as a Christian to honor God by relying on what we know *for sure* rather than depending upon other methods of guidance which at the very best are *unsure* and dependant on using Scripture out of context. None of us can be transformed in our thinking if we are out of His will. The only way to know His will confidently is to embrace a biblical view of guidance and to trust God's Word and His providence instead of trusting some vague, mysterious impression, "check," or still small voice that we think we may have heard or felt. If we are to be renewed in our thinking and attitudes then it follows that we must **"not be foolish but <u>understand</u> what the will of the Lord is"** (Ephesians 5:17; emphasis added).

∽

Chapter 7

Study Questions

1. What is the "Spirit-filled" life? In order to be "Spirit-filled," what must you be saturated with? See principle # 1 on page 103.

2. Give an example of how the typical unmarried unbeliever might view sex outside of marriage and how that same person's thinking would be different after he becomes a Christian.

3. What is wrong with this thought? - "It is always God's will for me to be happy and never suffer."

4. What is the only time a Christian must refuse to obey someone in authority over them?

5. How should we think about our circumstances and God's providence?

6. How could it be possible for a Christian to "feel" that something is right when it is, in fact, wrong?

7. According to principle # 2 on page 106, who are those people who are being led by the Spirit?

8. What do the Scriptures teach us to do instead of "sitting back and letting God?"

9. What is the context of Matthew 18:15-19?

10. What is wrong with being definite concerning God's will when we have an apparent "open door?"

11. According to the first paragraph under the "Conclusion" on page 109, how is it possible to think God is leading you (because of a feeling or desire you have) when that is not the case?

12. From the last paragraph in this chapter, what is the only way to confidently know God's will?

Chapter 8

Practical Application of Doctrine: Worship

As I would think about worshiping God before I became a Christian, three scenes came to mind. One was the Jewish religion in which the traditions were so wonderful, reverent, and seemingly worshipful. Another was the Roman Catholic religion in which the banners, robes, candles, and chants were compelling. The third scene that came to my mind when I thought of worship was the song, "Oh, worship the King, all glorious above..." And of course those who truly worshiped God had a gigantic, gold-edged Bible open for all to see in the middle of the coffee table in the living room!

Worship in my mind was outward show and somehow the people going through the motions were closer to God because of their piety than I was. However, since I have come to know the Lord and He has given me a capacity to begin to understand worship from a pure heart instead of a deceived heart, I have changed my mind. True worship is *not* an outward show of religion, however compelling. True worship *is* bowing in humility and awe before the only true God (the God of the Bible), praising Him, sacrificing for Him, and serving Him as He desires and deserves. *Worship goes on all the time in every thought we think and every act we perform.* We either glorify God or we do not. And it also goes without saying that worship occurs as well in the formal times of **"assembling of ourselves together"** (Hebrews 10:25).

Abraham's Sacrifice of Worship

The Bible tells a very gripping story of worship in the story of Abraham. Abraham was very old and living the life of a nomad moving from place to place. He had waited a long, long time for God to fulfill His promise that He would give him a son. Finally the day arrived when Sara gave birth to Isaac much to everyone's amazement! Several years later, God tested Abraham's trust and faith. The test was to take his son, Isaac, to Mount Moriah to worship God by building an altar and sacrificing Isaac — the beloved, promised son of Abraham's old age.

Abraham thought that after he offered the sacrifice, God was going to somehow raise Isaac from the dead (Hebrews 11:17-19). As Abraham instructed his servants to wait at the bottom of the mountain he said, **"Stay here with the donkey, and I and the lad will go yonder; and *we* will worship and return to you"** (Genesis 22:5, emphasis added). Imagine Abraham's emotions as he and Isaac walked on together when Isaac asked, **"...where is the lamb for the burnt offering?"** (Genesis 22:7). Abraham replied simply, **"God will provide for Himself the lamb for the burnt offering, my son"** (Genesis 22:8). And God did provide. Even as Abraham stretched out his arm with knife in hand to slay his son, the Lord stopped him, commended his obedience, and provided a ram in the place of Isaac. Abraham worshiped God with the most precious sacrifice that an elderly father could possibly have made, his beloved son.

God's Sacrifice of Worship

Two thousand years later, there was to be another sacrifice of another beloved Son. This time the sacrifice *would* be completed, and God's beloved Son, the Lord Jesus Christ, would die an agonizing, humiliating death on the cross as a living sacrifice for sin. He was *the* holy God/man, so His sacrifice was pure and perfectly acceptable to God.

Picture in your mind the glimpse into heavenly worship to which the Apostle John was privileged:

> *...and behold, a throne was standing in heaven, and One sitting on the throne And He who was sitting was like a jasper stone and a sardius in appearance; and there was a rainbow around the throne, like an emerald in appearance. Around the throne were twenty-four thrones; and upon the thrones I saw twenty-four elders sitting clothed in white garments, and golden crowns on their heads. And from the throne proceed flashes of lightning and sounds and peals of thunder. And there were seven lamps of fire burning before the throne, which are the seven Spirits of God; and before the throne there was, as it were, something like a sea of glass, like crystal; and in the center*

> *and around the throne, four living creatures full of eyes in front and behind. The first creature was like a lion, and the second creature like a calf, and the third creature had a face like that of a man, and the fourth creature was like a flying eagle; the four living creatures, each one of them having six wings, are full of eyes around and within; and day and night they do not cease to say, "Holy, holy, holy is the Lord God, the Almighty, who was and who is and who is to come." And when the living creatures give glory and honor and thanks to Him who sits on the throne, to Him who lives forever and ever, the twenty-four elders will fall down before Him who sits on the throne, and will worship Him who lives forever and ever, and will cast their crowns before the throne, saying, "Worthy are You, our Lord and our God, to receive glory and honor and power; for You created all things, and because of Your will they existed, and were created." Revelation 4:2-11*

Abraham worshiped God through obedience as he attempted to carry out the sacrifice of his son of promise, his beloved Isaac. Now God's creatures in heaven and the twenty-four elders are worshiping God through praise of His worth, adoring Him, and casting their crowns before His splendid throne in heaven. In heaven His glory is not hidden but on full display!

We know from Scripture that Abraham *did* worship God and that the elders in heaven are *currently* worshiping God, but what about us *now*? The only way to know if our worship is genuine and pleasing to God instead of merely outward religious show is to search the Scriptures and see if it is true to the Word of God. As we pursue a simple basic understanding of the doctrine of Worship, let's consider six basic principles concerning true, acceptable worship of God.

Six Basic Principles Concerning True Worship

1. We are to worship the one true God only.

> *Again the devil took Him to a very high mountain and showed Him all the kingdoms of the world and their glory; and he said to Him, "All these things I will give you, if You fall down and worship me." Then Jesus said to him,*

"Begone, Satan! For it is written, 'YOU SHALL WOR-SHIP THE LORD YOUR GOD, AND SERVE HIM ONLY.'"　　　　　　　　　　　*Matthew 4:8-10*

Come, let us worship and bow down, let us kneel before the LORD our Maker. For He is our God, and we are the people of His pasture and the sheep of His hand.　　　　　　　　　　　　　　　*Psalm 95:6-7*

When I think of worship, I am reminded of a painting I recently saw at the National Portrait Gallery in Washington, D.C. In the painting the Pilgrims were walking through the snowy woods in single file, Bibles in hand, on their way to their house of worship. The picture reminded me of how they lived a hard life amid harsh conditions. They fled from England and Holland so they could have the freedom to worship God as they saw fit. Many of them died early deaths. They knew what it was really like to depend on God their Maker each and every day for life and breath. They were grateful to God. From their writings we know that for most of them it was very important that they give God glory and honor. It is unlikely that those early Pilgrims were just going through an outward, ritualistic show of devotion and worship. They worshiped the God of the Scriptures, not some man-made conjured-up-version of God. They embraced God's love and mercy as well as His justice and holiness. They bowed before Him in humble contrition, utter dependence, love for Him, and trust of His goodness and rule over them. They proclaimed His worth and His excellencies through prayer, sermons, and song. Their adoration was in their hearts as well as in their outward simple practices. They longed to be holy. The pilgrims worshiped the one true God.

2.　True worshipers worship the Father in Spirit and in truth.

But an hour is coming, and now is, when the true worshipers will worship the Father in spirit and truth; for such people the Father seeks to be His worshipers. God is spirit, and those who worship Him must worship in spirit and truth.　　　　　　　　　　　　　　*John 4:23-24*

Perhaps you remember the context of the previous two verses. The Lord Jesus had stopped to rest in Samaria. While there several remarkable events happened. A Samaritan woman came to draw water from the well and the Lord Jesus asked her for a drink. Well, she was shocked that a Jewish man would speak to her much less ask her for a drink! So she asked Him why He was speaking to her. He replied, **"If you knew the gift of God, and who it is who**

says to you, 'Give me a drink,' you would have asked Him, and He would have given you living water" (John 4:10). Their conversation continued and she eventually did ask Him for the living water that gives eternal life.

The conversation took a dramatic turn as Jesus began to tell her about her sinful background, her five previous husbands and the man with whom she was currently living. She decided that He must be a prophet of God so she asked Him a religious question, "Where is the right place to worship - here in this mountain or in Jerusalem?" Jesus explained that it was neither, but that someday true believers would worship in **"spirit and truth** (John 4:24)**."** What happened next was even more astonishing as the Lord Jesus plainly told her that He was the prophesied Messiah. At that point, she put down her water pot and ran back to the city and told others to come and see this man who must be the Messiah because He had told her all that she had done.

One of the main points of this story is that the actual city or place in which you worship is not the issue. The issue is your heart's attitude before God. The "true worshipers" are those who are born again supernaturally by the Holy Spirit (John 3:3-5) and have been given a new heart by God so that they can, in turn, proclaim His excellencies and declare His worth in a way that will be pleasing to Him (Titus 3:5).

To worship **"in spirit"** means the human spirit (John 4:24). In other words, who we are on the inside. This understanding stands in vivid contrast to the external place of outward, ritual worship. Our worship will be sincere if we have a proper heart's attitude of humility and reverence for God. It will also be acceptable to God because we will have been cleansed from sin because of the death of Christ on the cross on our behalf (2 Corinthians 5:21). To worship **"in truth"**(John 4:24) simply means that the only valid way to worship God is through the Lord Jesus Christ as He would clearly explain later on in the Gospel of John, **"I am the way, and the truth, and the life; no one comes to the Father but through Me** (John 14:6)**."** Only true believers can worship God in **"spirit and truth** (John 4:24)**."** All other worship is futile and empty regardless of the place or the magnitude of the pomp.

3. Some religious people are worshiping the Lord Jesus Christ in vain.

> *[Jesus said to the Pharisees] You hypocrites, rightly did Isaiah prophesy of you: "This people honors Me with their lips, but their heart is far away from Me. But in vain do they worship Me, teaching as doctrines the precepts of men."*   Matthew 15:7-9, explanation added

There is probably not a church anywhere that does not have traditions. Their worship service usually follows the same basic pattern every Sunday. In each and every service, members of the congregation raise their voice in song, bow their heads in prayer, perhaps partake of communion, or observe a baptism, and listen to the sermon. Some stand and repeat the Lord's prayer every Sunday. Some stand and sing the "Doxology" every week just after collecting the offering. All of these forms of worship are certainly not in and of themselves wrong, but what the people are thinking in their hearts (minds) as they go about their traditions can mean the difference between mere outward lip service and true worship.

When what we believe about what we are singing, saying, and hearing in worship is not true to the Scriptures, it becomes a teaching of men. A precept is a general principle and in this case it is a principle that is made up by men. For example, some believe that man must earn his salvation by doing good works. Another example is that man receives special grace from God by taking communion each Sunday. If he misses communion, he becomes back-slidden and loses his salvation. Some churches teach that the Bible has errors and you must pick and choose which parts are true and which parts are not true. Others give lip service to prayer but do not pray in Jesus' name because they believe Jesus to be a man just like any other. The list could go on and on but the point is that men (due to their spiritual blindness) make up doctrines that are not acceptable to God. Many live their entire lives faithfully attending church and serving diligently in their church, yet their efforts are all in vain. Their thoughts and beliefs must be biblically accurate or their worship is sadly meaningless. What may outwardly look like splendid worship in reality is a room full of hearts far away from God.

4. We are to worship God and sing His praises for His awesome works.

> *Shout joyfully to God, all the earth; sing the glory of His name, make His praise glorious. Say to God, "How awesome are Your works! Because of the greatness of Your power Your enemies will give feigned obedience to You, all the earth will worship You, and will sing praises to You; they will sing praises to Your name." Come and see the works of God, who is awesome in His deeds towards the sons of men.* **Psalm 66:1-5**

My computer has a feature called a screen saver. When I do not change anything on the screen for a certain number of minutes, the screen saver comes on in order to prevent damage to the screen. My husband loaded into my computer various pictures such as a waterfall scene or a magnificent mountain range. One of the pictures is an entire screen full of incredible pink roses. The picture is exceedingly beautiful and even though I have seen it many times, it still gives me pause for thought. My thought is – look what God has done and what He has given us to enjoy! The creation is one of the works of God.

Other works of God are His miracles recorded in the Scriptures for us. For example, **"He turned the sea into dry land; they passed through the river on foot..."** (Psalm 66:6). His works also include His rule over us and His providential care to guide, sustain, and mold us into His image. **"He rules by His might forever...Who keeps us in life and does not allow our feet to slip. For You have tried us, O God; you have refined us as silver is refined"** (Psalm 66:7,9,10). Last, but certainly not least, is God's work on our behalf for salvation. The Psalmist expressed it this way, **"Come and hear, all who fear God, and I will tell of what He has done for my soul"** (Psalm 66:16). For all these works and more, we are to worship God and gratefully sing His praises.

5.   We are to worship the LORD with reverence.

> *Worship the LORD with reverence and rejoice with trembling.*   *Psalm 2:11*

About eighteen years ago I was almost killed in an automobile accident. When I regained consciousness I could not breathe. I realized that I was likely going to pass out again and shortly thereafter I was going to die. During those few moments all I thought about was the Lord Jesus and what He would be like when I saw Him. I remembered parts of the verses in 2 Corinthians 5:6-8.

> *Therefore, being always of good courage, and knowing that while we are at home in the body we are absent from the Lord - for we walk by faith, not by sight – we are of good courage, I say, and prefer rather to be absent from the body and to be at home with the Lord.*

As I sat temporarily trapped in that car and still unable to breathe, I tried to imagine what He would be like when I saw Him — face to face. Instead of dying and seeing the Lord, I began to breathe again, but I have often thought about that moment and how close I thought I was to death and heaven. I was a young Christian and wanted to be right there with Him in the front row! Now that I have known the Lord for over twenty years, I still wonder what it would be like to see Him. Now, however, when I think of seeing Him I am much more in awe of being in His presence. I think that seeing the Lord Jesus in His full glory will overwhelm me. It makes me want to quietly and reverently sneak into heaven, get on the very back row, and then peek at the Lord. The very thought of it makes me almost tremble.

The glimpse that we have now of our Lord Jesus is through His Word. It should not take an automobile wreck to make us think reverent thoughts about our Lord. Instead each time we read His Word, pray to Him, or participate in corporate worship with our church family, we should be worshiping Him with reverence. As we worship Him today, our thoughts and emotions should begin to prepare us for the fullness of the experience when we are with Him.

6. We have an obligation to worship God through living totally devoted to Him.

> *Therefore I urge you, brethren, by the mercies of God, to present your bodies a living and holy sacrifice, acceptable to God, which is your spiritual service of worship.*
> *Romans 12:1*

Earlier in this chapter we learned about Abraham's near sacrifice of his beloved son, Isaac. Here in Romans chapter twelve, God (through the Apostle Paul) is calling *us* to be a *living* and *holy* sacrifice so that we may worship God in a way that is pleasing to Him.

A sacrifice is when you give up something for someone or something else. In other words you place that person or thing above yourself. For example, I might forego sleeping in on a Saturday morning in order to take my grandchildren to the park. (Obviously, taking my grandbabies to the park is not a great personal sacrifice but being a living sacrifice for the Lord Jesus may be.) The dead animals sacrificed in the Old Testament were to have been the very best their owner had to offer. What God requires of us has not changed, but the sacrifices have and they are to come from, not a dead animal, but a living, breathing, born again Christian.

The sacrifice of ourselves for the Lord is not a vague, elusive concept. Neither is it dependent on some sort of feeling. It is a sacrifice of your body as well as your mind (which is part of your body). It is what you *do*, however mundane every day. It is also what you *think about* what you are doing as well as your *attitudes and motives*. It may be as simple as being stopped for a red light and, yet, thanking God for the delay. It may be as complicated as the tragic and unexpected death of a loved one, and yet thanking God for the time that He allowed you to have him or her.

A living sacrifice is holy and pure. It includes a whole heart's desire to serve and please God and to be used by Him for His purposes however He chooses. Second best won't do. It must and can only be the best because of **"the mercies of God"** (Romans 12:1). God's mercies include saving us and giving us a new heart with desires to serve Him and give Him glory. They also include God's power to obey His Word and repent of our sin. His mercies include His grace to us without which we can do nothing that is acceptable to Him. Being a living sacrifice is much more than just attending church or teaching Sunday School. It is a daily sacrifice of self for what God would require of you.

Conclusion

Worship is not outward pomp, traditions, candles, or chants. It is extolling God's worth. It is expressing through words, thoughts, or music adoration of God Most High. It is living a life (because of God's mercies) as a holy and pure sacrifice that desires God's will and pleasure more than you desire your own. It does occur on Sunday but it is also on-going in our hearts and outward actions every day. It is a preview of the magnificently grand worship that is (even as I write) occurring in heaven.

> *...and day and night they [the living creatures] do not cease to say, "Holy, holy, holy is the Lord God, the Almighty, who was and who is and who is to come." And when the living creatures give glory and honor and thanks to Him who sits on the throne, to Him who lives forever and ever, the twenty-four elders will fall down before Him who sits on the throne, and will worship Him who lives forever and ever, and will cast their crowns before the throne, saying, "Worthy are You, our Lord and our God, to receive glory and honor and power; for You created all things, and because of Your will they existed, and were created."*   Revelation 4:8-11, explanation added

❦

Chapter 8

Study Questions

1. According to Hebrews 11:17-19, what was Abraham thinking as he and his son, Isaac, walked up Mount Moriah to worship God?

2. What did the Lord Jesus reply to the Devil when the Devil wanted Jesus to worship him?

3. Who are the "true worshipers?"

4. What does it mean to worship "in spirit?"

5. What does it mean to worship "in truth?"

6. How is it that a religious person could faithfully attend church and yet be worshiping God in vain?

7. Make a list of the works of God. Take a few minutes to pray and thank Him for what He has done and is doing.

8. According to Psalm 2:11, what should our attitude be when we worship the Lord?

9. What kind of sacrifice are we to be for God? See Romans 12:1.

10. Describe in your own words what it means to be a "living sacrifice" for the Lord.

Part Three

Attitudes of Heart

Blessed are the pure in heart,
for they shall see God.
Matthew 5:8

Chapter 9

Thoughts and Attitudes

Imagine yourself singing in the church choir. The song is somewhat challenging, especially since it is to be sung without the musical instruments. Also it is very fast-paced and the timing is tricky. In spite of all the obstacles, you are not worried but enjoying this opportunity to sing to the Lord. After all, you went to the choir practices and practiced privately at home. During the performance everything is going well until you accidentally look at the wrong line. As a result, you sing out a phrase before anyone else. You quickly realize what you are doing and stop singing but it is very likely that some of the choir members heard you as well as the people on the first few rows of the church. You can feel the pace of your heart speed up and your face begin to turn a deep crimson color. What do you suppose you would think at such an embarrassing moment?

You might think, "I am so embarrassed. I will never sing in the choir again." You also might think, "Oh, I am so frustrated!" or "What will other people think?" or "I bet they are laughing at me." Or "I hate this, let me out of here." Tears begin to well up in your eyes and as if singing an unplanned solo isn't bad enough, now you can't see the music clearly and your nose starts to run. All you can think about during the rest of the church service is what happened and how others must think badly of you. You cannot wait to get out of there. When you get home, you continue to think about your embarrassing episode but then your thinking changes for the worse (if that is possible). Somehow, it becomes the fault of the choir director who cancelled the extra practice or the fault of the church members who are (in your mind) making fun of you. After an agonizing night of being unable to sleep due to thinking about the entire situation, you decide that you will never go back to that church again.

Now, let's think this same scene through but with different thoughts. Imagine yourself singing in the church choir. The song is somewhat challenging especially since it is to be sung without the musical instruments. Also it is very fast-paced and the timing is tricky. In spite of all the obstacles, you are not worried but enjoying this opportunity to sing to the Lord. After all, you went to the choir practices and practiced privately at home. During the performance everything is going well until you accidentally look at the wrong line. As a result, you sing out a phrase before anyone else. You quickly realize what you are doing and stop singing but it is very likely that some of the choir members heard you as well as the people on the first few rows of the church. You can feel the pace of your heart speed up and your face begin to turn a deep crimson color. What do you suppose you would think at such an embarrassing moment?

Of course you feel uncomfortable and wish you could disappear out of the choir or perhaps disappear off the face of the earth, but you think, "This is not the end of the world. I can continue to sing. In fact I am going to continue to sing whether I make another mistake or not. If I have to feel embarrassed again, I'll just have to feel embarrassed; but I am going to sing for the Lord." Even though you feel embarrassed and your face has turned a little red, you continue to sing and you do not feel as if you are going to cry. Therefore you can still see clearly and your nose does not begin to run. When the choir is dismissed and you sit down for the sermon, the unintentional solo is still on your mind. So, you pray, "Lord thank you for the opportunity once more to be reminded of how fallible I am and how perfect You are. I love You and pray that I will be permitted by You to sing your praises the best that I can. I pray that this mistake will be used by You to give You glory. Help me to be humble and not sinfully proud. In Jesus Name, Amen." After that you are able to concentrate on the sermon and by the time you get home, you have all but forgotten your ill-timed solo.

How is it that someone could go through the same exact circumstance twice and have such a completely different attitude? How could they sin horribly one time and the other time give God great glory? Obviously it was because of how they *thought* about their mistake. Their thoughts resulted in either a wicked, self-focused heart and sinful attitude or their thoughts resulted in an opportunity to give God glory and to recover from the goof-up quickly.

In order to have right thoughts, you must first be placed in a position by God to give Him glory. You can give God glory only after you have been regenerated by the Holy Spirit (given a new heart by God at the moment of your salvation) and you are also given the enabling grace of God to think and respond in a righteous manner (Ephesians 2:8-9).

When one of our granddaughters was three years old, she had the attitude that she was the most important child in the family. In fact, I believe she thought she was the most important person in the entire world! When all the children were called to come to receive a snack or a surprise, she would come quickly yelling, "Me first, me first!" One day I asked her if her philosophy of life was "Me first, I'm better" and she said, with a huge smile, "Yes!" It is debatable whether she understood what I was talking about, but she appeared quite confident in her assertion. Her attitude of being better and wanting to be first came from what she was thinking. Instead of being content, grateful, humble, loving, forebearing, and serving, she wanted to be preeminent and always first. When she was not first, her little countenance fell and often she would frown, poke her lip out, cross her arms, toss her curly blonde hair in anger, and burst into tears. Her sinful attitude came from what she was thinking and resulted in outward sin. Just like my granddaughter, our attitudes begin with what we are thinking. Assuming that you are a Christian and have the Holy Spirit to help you transform your thinking, I want to begin with an explanation of some biblical principles regarding right thinking.

Four Biblical Principles Regarding Right Thinking

1. To have right thinking you must have right presuppositions about God.

   > *Before the mountains were born, or You gave birth to the earth and the world, even from everlasting to everlasting, You are God.*   *Psalm 90:2*

   > *That they may know that You alone, whose name is the LORD, are the Most High over all the earth.*
   >   *Psalm 83:18*

   > *To whom would you liken Me and make Me equal and compare Me, that we would be alike? ... Remember the former things long past, for I am God, and there is no other; I am God, and there is no one like Me.*
   >   *Isaiah 46:5,9*

   Before you drive a car, you have presuppositions. A presupposition about driving is what you assume to be true about driving a car before you ever back out of the driveway. You likely think that (Lord willing) the car will run well on the entire trip. You decide that the gas in your tank is sufficient to get you where you are going. You also assume that the other drivers will stay on their side of the road! If you didn't anticipate a good trip, obviously you wouldn't drive. Just like driving a car, we have preconceived beliefs about most subjects. It is the same way with what you believe about God. For example, an atheist presupposes there is no God. Many pagans believe there are multiple gods. Some believe that they are God or that they will *become* God! You see, we all have preconceived ideas (whether right or wrong) about everything that goes on around us.

God does not want us to have *wrong* presuppositions about Him. He has chosen to reveal Himself to us specifically today through His Word. It is through God's Word that we learn, for example, that God is eternal, the Creator of heaven and earth, and there is no other god like Him. Our thoughts about God must always be in accordance with the Scriptures. Otherwise our thoughts will be wrong and consequently our attitudes will be wrong. Again, if I presuppose that God owes me a favor due to the hard work I do on His behalf and then something bad happens in my life, I might think, "Look how I have served God all these years and this is the thanks I get!" Certainly the attitude that will follow such beliefs and thoughts would be incredible ungratefulness and massive sinful pride. On the other hand, if I presuppose that God is not indebted to me and something bad happens in my life, I might think, "This is hard, but God is testing me to give me a special opportunity to glorify *Him*." The resultant attitude will be one of gratitude to the Lord and humility that God is using me. So you can see that what we presuppose to be true about God is critical to what we think and our heart's attitude.

2. To have right thinking you must have a proper regard for God's Word.

> *For this reason we also constantly thank God that when you received the word of God which you heard from us [Paul, Silvanus, and Timothy], you accepted it <u>not as the word of men, but for what it really is, the word of God</u>, which also performs its work in you who believe.*
> *1 Thessalonians 2:13, explanation and emphasis added*

> *...for you have been born again not of seed which is perishable but imperishable, that is, through the living and abiding word of God. For, "All flesh is like grass, and all its glory like the flower of grass. The grass withers, and the flower falls off, <u>but the word of the LORD abides forever</u>."*   *1 Peter 1:23-25, emphasis added*

For the word of God is living and active and sharper than any two-edged sword, and piercing as far as the division of soul and spirit, of both joints and marrow, and able to judge the thoughts and intentions of the heart.

Hebrews 4:12

When you hear a choir sing "How Great Thou Art," your emotions soar as you think of God and how truly great He is. When you see the magnificent paintings of a master painter, you exclaim "How wonderful!" When you touch the cloth of an extraordinary weaver of fabric, you think, "How perfect!" It is easy to see that all three have been given gifts by God to display their talent. You might even have the thought, "They were inspired by God." But if you look carefully you will find flaws in the music, paintings, and fabric. Some people are most certainly gifted by God to display amazing talent and are inspired in some sense to produce exceptional products, but none of them are inspired the way the Word of God is inspired. They don't even come in a distant second.

The Scriptures, however, are perfectly God-inspired (2 Timothy 3:16-17). Its prophecies were not made **"by an act of human will, but men moved by the Holy Spirit spoke from God"** (2 Peter 1:21). They are God's Word without error. God is perfect and therefore so is His Word. It is His Word and only His Word that is **"perfect and restores the soul..."** (Psalm 19:7). We must think rightly about God's Word so that we will look to the God-inspired, perfect Scriptures to learn how to think rightly.

As our thinking changes, we will develop a biblical perspective on life and the world. In other words, we will develop a biblical frame of reference.

<u>Let the word of Christ richly dwell within you</u>, with all wisdom teaching and admonishing one another with psalms and hymns an spiritual songs, singing with thankfulness in your hearts to God. Whatever you do in word or deed, do all in the name of the Lord Jesus, giving thanks through Him to God the Father.

Colossians 3:16-17, emphasis added

When a surveyor stakes out a house that is to be built on a lot, he places stakes with red flags where the four corners of the house are to be placed. Next, he places three additional stakes with green flags outside of each corner stake. The purpose of the additional stakes is to give a frame of reference for the actual four corners while the bulldozers are clearing the land for the house. Just as the green stakes give the bulldozer driver a frame of reference for the place-ment of the future house, the Word of God gives us a biblical frame of reference on which to develop our beliefs and values.

For example, one belief upon which feminists place great value is that a woman has a right to choose to do with her body what she pleases. Her choice may on occasion include aborting her unborn child. In contrast, the Scriptural belief upon which Christians place value is the sanctity of life because life is a precious gift from God and we are created in the image of God (Genesis 9:6). Therefore, we are not to commit murder. All people make decisions based on what they believe and what they value. In order for Christians to develop bib-lical beliefs and values they must first **"Let the Word of Christ richly dwell within [them]"** (Colossians 3:16) through reading, meditating upon, and study-ing the Scriptures so that what God values and believes will become their frame of reference instead of what the world values and believes.

3. To have right thinking your mind must be renewed.

> *And do not be conformed to this world, but be transformed by the renewing of your mind, so that you may prove what the will of God is, that which is good and acceptable and perfect.* **Romans 12:2**

The non-Christian people of the world do not for the most part think as we do. Often, their thoughts and resulting beliefs are the opposite of how God, through His Word, instructs us to think and believe. One vivid example is my former belief in evolution. I can remember as early as the fifth or sixth grade being introduced to the theory of evolution. That was over forty years ago. From the fifth grade on, learning about evolution became a yearly routine in school. High School only reinforced the teaching, and college (especially for the science major I was) entrenched my belief in evolution to the point of my having an unshakable faith in a theory that I thought would eventually be proven to be true.

A few weeks after I became a Christian, I was driving home from my job where I taught nursing students and I started thinking about the theory of evo-lution. I thought about the pictures you see in the science books of the progres-sion from ape to man. On the left side of the page there is a drawing of an ape. As he moves across the page, he begins to stand up and gradually look more and more like a man. By the time he is ready to walk off the right side of the page he has become a stone-age man, but a man nevertheless. As I thought about that evolutionary sequence, it suddenly occurred to me, "That's not true! It never happened! God created man and the animals and the entire creation was finished in six days!" I was so excited that when I got home I told my husband, Sanford, "Guess what? You know those evolutionary sequences in the science books that begin as an ape and end up a man? It never happened! God created man!" Sanford replied, "Of course it never happened! Where have you been?" And I answered, "In science class at Georgia State University." My mind had been deceived into believing a lie. It took the Spirit of God and the Word of God to renew my mind to think rightly about the origin of man.

As a new Christian, the transformation of my mind concerning evolution was only beginning. Twenty years later, it still continues. God provides the grace through His Word and the Holy Spirit's illumination of God's Word as truth. Transforming your thinking is also a command to all believers, **"Do *not* be conformed to this world, but be transformed by the renewing of your *mind* ...**(Romans 12:2, emphasis added). Your mind must be renewed if you are going to have right thinking, but be aware that there is a battle for the mind.

> *For though we walk in the flesh, <u>we do not war accord-
ing to the flesh, for the weapons of our warfare are not of
the flesh, but divinely powerful</u> for the destruction of for-
tresses. We are destroying speculations and every lofty
thing raised up against the knowledge of God, and <u>we
are taking every thought captive to the obedience of
Christ,</u> and we are ready to punish all disobedience, when-
ever your obedience is complete.*
> *2 Corinthians 10:3-6, emphasis added*

When I think of a battle and war, I cannot help but think of the song, "Onward Christian Soldiers." Part of the song goes, "This through countless ages, men and angels sing...Onward Christian soldiers, marching as to war..."[38] When I think about marching off to war, I think about my children's church class of more than a dozen four, five, and six year olds. One Sunday after their snack, it was time to take them all to the restroom which was down a long hall on the opposite end of the building. So, I thought we would make the trek fun. I lined the children up and with me at the front of the line, we marched down the hall all the while singing a rousing rendition of the song "Onward Christian Soldiers!" Nursery workers' heads were popping out of doors to see what the commotion was all about but like good little soldiers we kept marching straight ahead for our mission. Once our mission was accomplished we marched back the same way we had come. Our mission was a routine, although fun, trek. On the contrary, God's soldiers are fighting an entirely different kind of battle and it is real and very serious.

The battle that God's soldiers fight is for their minds to think the way that God would have them think – taking their wrong thoughts captive out of respect and obedience to their Lord, Jesus Christ. Thoughts, ideas, speculations, reasonings, philosophies, and false religions are our battle.[39] It is a battle that is daily and ongoing until we go to be with the Lord. It is a battle that is fought by means of God's power through prayer and study of the Scriptures. The results are a renewed mind that thinks rightly, thus taking **"every thought captive to the obedience of Christ"** (2 Corinthians 10:5).

One of the ways that, by God's grace, we develop a renewed mind is by preparing ahead of time what we are going to think during a difficult situation.

> *Therefore, <u>prepare your minds for action</u>, keep sober in spirit, fix your hope completely on the grace to be brought to you at the revelation of Jesus Christ.*
> *1 Peter 1:13, emphasis added*

The apostle Peter wrote his letter (1 Peter) to Christians scattered throughout various Roman provinces. The persecution against Christians had heated up and would eventually become extreme. There is tremendous hope in Peter's letter that must have sent their emotions soaring as he wrote about the **"precious blood, as of a Lamb unblemished and spotless, the blood of Christ"** (I Peter 1:19). There is also a very sobering call to prepare mentally for the coming persecution and in the meantime to live a holy life entrusting their souls to their **"faithful Creator in doing what is right"** (1 Peter 4:19). Peter was trying to prepare them ahead of time so that when the trials came they would think rightly through them and give God great glory. It was as if Peter was telling them, "I have some really bad news and you need to prepare yourself for it – great persecution is coming and God will test your faith to see if it is genuine. He will give some of you a great privilege to suffer for His sake. You need to think about this now so that you will honor our Lord when the time actually comes."

Fearful people do not trust God. Instead of thinking through a possible future difficulty **"fixing their hope completely on the grace to be brought to them,"** they let their thoughts wallow in the negative what-ifs (1 Peter 1:13). "What if this happens? What if that happens? I won't be able to bear it. I can't take it! I just know something horrible is going to happen!!" They worry and fret and panic about things that usually don't happen. Instead they should think that if a difficult or even extreme circumstance occurs, God is all powerful and faithful to keep His promises. Therefore, they can trust God completely knowing He would give them the grace they would need if such a difficulty arose. He is so good. He will not let His children be **"tempted beyond what [they] are**

able to bear" (1 Corinthians 10:13, adaptation added). Therefore (as Peter said), prepare your mind through trusting God, and in the meanwhile live a godly, righteous life.

4. To have right thinking you must *put off* wrong thoughts and *put on* godly thoughts.

> *...in reference to your former manner of life, you lay aside the old self, which is being corrupted in accordance with the lusts of deceit, and that you be renewed in the spirit of your mind, and put on the new self, which in the likeness of God has been created in righteousness and holiness of the truth.*   **Ephesians 4:22-24**

When you think a thought it is either pleasing to God or it is not. It is either righteous or it is not. If you think the same or similar thought often enough, it becomes a habit. We all think habitually. For example, when you first learned to brush your teeth you had to think carefully about everything you were doing – pick up the tooth brush, squeeze a little toothpaste on the toothbrush, place the toothbrush in your mouth and brush up and down, front and back, across the tops ... At first, brushing your teeth took tremendous thought concentration. You worked hard at it. Your motive was probably to please your mother who seemed to think that clean teeth were especially important. Gradually, brushing your teeth became easier and easier until now you can probably brush your teeth without looking in a mirror and at the same time think about something entirely unrelated. That is because you think habitually.

Thinking habitually can be good or bad. On the positive side, you can perform functions in life (such as dressing yourself) with relative ease. On the down side, you have also trained yourself to think sinful thoughts. For example, suppose as a child you woke up in the middle of the night and heard a noise. You thought, "There is a monster in my room and he is going to get me!" As a result, you felt very frightened and called for your mother. Or suppose that as a child your older brother was mean to you one day and you thought, "I hate him. I'll show him what it's like!" As a result, you felt very frustrated and you grabbed your doll and hit your brother over the head as hard as you could. Children think fearful or angry thoughts because they are sinners. The longer children live, the more they think sinful thoughts. The sinful thoughts become easier and easier to think. They become a habit. The child grows up thinking the same kind of sinful thoughts, although their outward reactions are likely more adult-like than child-like. Regardless, their thoughts are sinful and the

Scripture says that Christians are to *put them off*.

In order to put off sinful thoughts, the Christian must stop thinking the sinful thoughts by replacing them with righteous, godly thoughts. Consider the child who was afraid of the monster. Instead of thinking, "I just know the monster is in here," she could have thought, "There are no such things as monsters, and when I am afraid I will trust in God." Or what about the little girl who became so enraged at her brother that she bonked him on the head with her doll baby. Instead of thinking, "I hate him!" she could have thought, "He is sinning. How can I overcome evil with good?" Children do not naturally think the righteous way. This wrong thinking is not because they are children, rather it is because they are sinners. Christian parents must train them to rethink their thoughts and actions in a way that pleases God. As they grow up, they will realize more and more that even if they try very hard they cannot please God without His help. His help means they must be saved and given a new heart by God with the accompanying new desires to please Him. Those new desires to please God, coupled with God's grace to help them think righteously, are just the beginning of the process of putting on the new self. There is no quick fix. It takes work on the part of the Christian that is only possible through God's enabling grace.

The new self thinks the God-pleasing thought immediately upon waking to a strange noise or being provoked by another person. How long and intensely they have thought the wrong kind of sinful thoughts will have a bearing on how long it will take to replace the habitual, automatic sinful thoughts with habitual, automatic God-pleasing and God-honoring thoughts. Scripture is clear, the fear will not subside until we trust God. The anger will not go away until we are kind, tender-hearted, and forgiving. We are to *put off* wrong thoughts with God's help by *putting on* righteous thoughts.[40]

Wrong, sinful thoughts do not descend upon us out of the blue. They begin with our sinful heart.

> *You brood of vipers, how can you, being evil, speak what is good? For the mouth speaks out of that which fills the heart. The good man brings out of his good treasure what is good; and the evil man brings out of his evil treasure what is evil.*　　　　　*Matthew 12:34-35*

> *Jesus said, "Are you also still without understanding? Do you not understand that everything that goes into the mouth passes into the stomach, and is eliminated? But the things that proceed out of the mouth come from the*

*heart, and those defile the man. For out of the heart come
evil thoughts, murders, adulteries, fornications, thefts,
false witness, slanders. These are the things which defile
the man; but to eat with unwashed hands does not defile
the man."*   *Matthew 15:16-20*

The Pharisees were deceived. They thought that their hand-washing routine made them clean and undefiled before God. The Lord Jesus explained, however, that it was their hearts, not their hands, which were defiling them. Their hearts were who they were on the inside. It included their thoughts, motives, and choices. The problem started on the inside with what they thought. The result was outward obvious sin.

Inward sin tends to escalate like a snowball rolling down a hill. Those watching the snowball roll probably cannot even see it at first but by the time it reaches the bottom of the hill it is so large that it is obvious to everyone. Consider for instance King Saul's attitude towards David. When Saul first met David, **"Saul loved him greatly, and he became his armor bearer"** (1 Samuel 16:21). Well, David killed Goliath and after that whenever Saul sent David out to battle, the Lord prospered David and gave him victory. The women began to sing of David's victories and he became very popular. Saul should have been glad for David but instead he **"became *very angry*...and looked at David with *suspicion* from that day on"** because he thought that David would try to take his kingdom from him (1 Samuel 18:8-9, emphasis added). Saul had no proof of anything other than complete loyalty on David's part, but what started out as love for David became (due to Saul's change of thinking) hatred that escalated into Saul's attempting to murder David. King Saul, like the Pharisees, had an obvious, outward sin problem. But his outward sin began with what he thought. Sinful thought patterns begin with a sinful heart.

One example of thought patterns that begin with a sinful heart is daydreaming.

> *For in many dreams and in many words there is empti-*
> *ness. Rather, fear God.*   *Ecclesiastes 5:7*

Television commercials often portray a dream vacation on some exotic island. As you watch the pictures of the beach and the crystal clear water, you can imagine yourself strolling along the beach holding hands with the man of your dreams while talking to each other in an animated, earnest way as he looks into your eyes with a look that says, "I adore you!" As your day continues, your mind wanders back to the daydream of the romantic beach episode and you smile at the thought until reality sets in when your husband comes home from work tired, dirty, and grouchy. As a result of your off-and-on day-dream all day and your husband's less than romantic homecoming from work, you feel very hurt and very unhappy. Your daydream has definitely affected your emotions and your attitude toward your husband. Instead of preferring your husband over yourself and showing love to him, you feel cheated and your response to your husband is unkind and irritable.

What else do women daydream about besides great romance? Often they daydream about past grudges and play those hurts in vivid detail over and over in their minds. Some daydream in a covetous, envious way about the house or clothing they wish they could have. Some daydream about being beautiful or famous. Some daydream about food and what they can eat next! The Scripture warns us against daydreaming. It says that it is empty and vain. We are to think on thoughts that are true and right and God-honoring. Instead of day-dreaming we are to fear God.

As we turn from empty daydreams to God-glorifying thoughts, it would benefit us to learn how to build our thinking around the qualities in Philippians 4:8.

> **Finally, brethren, whatever is true, whatever is honor-able, whatever is right, whatever is pure, whatever is lovely, whatever is of good repute, if there is any excel-lence and if anything worthy of praise, let your mind dwell on these things.** **Philippians 4:8**

When I was an instructor of nursing students at a junior college I had a criteria checklist by which to grade my students' clinical activity. For instance, one of the criteria was that they were on time. Another was that they under-stood their patient's medicines and side effects. Another was that they accurately administered the medicine to their patients. By the end of the shift, my students had either met each criterion or they had not. I would add up their score to determine whether they had passed or failed. The criteria for what kinds of thoughts we are to think is similar to the standard for the nursing students in that God has given us clear guidelines for how we are to think — true thoughts, right thoughts, pure thoughts, etc. God, however, does not grade us on a man-made scale. He demands perfection. He wants every one of our thoughts to please Him and honor Him. Yet He knows we cannot do this with-out His Word to guide us and His grace to help us.

Our obligation is to develop our thinking by building the qualities that Paul listed in Philippians 4:8. For example, a *true* thought is one that you know to be a fact and that reflects reality. If I think, "God hates me and He won't help me with my problem. I can't live like this any more!" that is simply not a true thought and does not accept the reality of what Scripture tells us about God and how He **"granted to us everything pertaining to life and godliness..."** (2 Peter 1:3). Instead I should think, "This is really difficult but God will give me the grace to go through it."

Another of the criteria for godly thoughts is that they be *honorable*. That is, worthy of respect and not trivial. In other words, they are honoring to God. They seem to go along with thoughts that are excellent and worthy of praise. These are all thoughts that point to God and give Him the glory. If I think, "Look at all I have done for God and this is the thanks I get!" my thought is self-focused instead of God-honoring and God-focused. It is pointing to myself and giving myself glory instead of God. It is self-serving and very sinful. Instead, I am to think God-honoring, excellent, and praise-worthy thoughts such as, "Thank You for letting me serve You. What else can I do for You, Lord, that would please You even if it means I must suffer in some way?"

In addition to true and God-honoring thoughts, we are to think thoughts that are *right*. What is right is spelled out clearly in the Bible along with what is wrong. If I think, "I'll take these towels out of the motel. No one will ever know", that is clearly not right. Instead, it is stealing and being a thief. If I think, "What she has done has hurt me so badly, I will never forgive her!" that too is not right. It is wicked and sinful bitterness and seeking revenge in your heart. Instead, our thoughts are to be right according to what has been determined by God.

Our thoughts are also to be *pure*. A pure thought does not lead to lust. If I daydream a romantic fantasy, my thoughts will not be pure; they will be impure and sinful. I must instead repent and think thoughts that do not lead to sinful lust. When I do think about other people, I am to think thoughts that are lovely and thus promote the best for the other person. In addition, my thoughts are to be *good repute* (or good report) thoughts that do not promote slander. For example, if you think, "She doesn't like me. She thinks she is better than I am because when I smiled at her and said hello, she didn't even look up." From there, you begin to think about telling your friends about the new lady at church who thinks she is better than everyone else. Obviously if you did, you would be spreading a bad report. Instead, you should have assumed the best about her to begin with, such as "Perhaps she did not hear me when I spoke to her. I need to make more effort to make her feel comfortable and welcomed." Then your thought would promote the best instead of the worst for the other person. And in the event that you realize that she really is being outwardly rude, you should think, "How can I help her to not be so rude? I'll try to become her friend and then talk with her (instead of talk with others) about it."

With my nursing students, I had some freedom to grade them as less-than-perfect and still pass them. But with God's criteria for how we are to think, there is no acceptable, less-than-perfect score (James 2:10). We either meet God's perfect standard in what we think or we do not. All of God's standards are high and holy and every thought we think is no exception. We are by His grace to build our thinking around the qualities listed in Philippians 4:8 and thus put off our wrong thoughts by putting on godly thoughts.

Conclusion

Remember the lady who sang in the choir at the beginning of the chapter? One time after her embarrassing episode she agonized so much that she eventually left the church. The other time, she thought God-honoring thoughts and quickly recovered. In one instance, she had a humble servant's heart. In the other instance, she had the self-serving heart's attitude of a prima donna who was more concerned about herself than she was about God and serving Him. Her attitude came from what she was thinking — either right thinking about God, others, and herself, or sinful thinking in violation of several of the biblical principles that we have seen in this chapter.

The Lord Jesus said, **"for out of the *heart* come evil thoughts, murders, adulteries, fornications, thefts, false witness, slanders. These are the things which defile the man; but to eat with unwashed hands does not defile the man"** (Matthew 15:19-20, emphasis added). As we said earlier, the heart is who you are on the inside. It is comprised of your thoughts, choices, and motives. Your thoughts must be righteous. You are accountable before God for each and every one of them. What you think will then determine whether your attitudes are honoring and pleasing to God or not. Before you go on to the next chapter, what is your prayer?

Chapter 9

Study Questions

1. How has God chosen to reveal Himself to us today?

2. Match the following:

God's Word is **"perfect and restores the soul."**	**Hebrews 4:12**
"... you accepted it not as the word of men, but for what it really is, the Word of God."	**1 Peter 1:23-25**
"The Word of God is ... able to judge the thoughts and intentions of the heart."	**1 Thessalonians 2:13**
"The Word of the LORD abides forever."	**Psalm 19:7**

3. From reading Colossians 3:16-17, what are we to let richly dwell within us?

4. Give two examples of a biblical belief or value.

5. According to the first paragraph on page 134, what is the battle that the Christian fights? How is it fought?

6. How did Peter warn Christians to prepare for persecution? See 1 Peter 4:13-19.

7. From Ephesians 4:22-24, you are to lay aside the _____ self, be renewed in the spirit of your _____, and put on the _____ self.

8. Why is thinking habitually good news or bad news? Explain.

9. Complete the "Put-Off and Put-On" Bible study in the addendum in the back of this book.

10. What did the Pharisees think made them clean before God? What did the Lord Jesus Christ say defiled them? See Matthew 15:16-20.

11. Instead of being angry at and suspicious of David, what should have been King Saul's attitude?

12. What do you daydream about that is vain or empty?

13. For each of the empty daydreams that you listed in question # 12, write out a detailed plan of what you will turn your thoughts to the next time you find yourself thinking wrongly.

14. Replace the following thoughts using the criteria from Philippians 4:8:
    a. "Why doesn't God help me? Look what He does for others."

    b. "If God were good, He wouldn't let me suffer like this."

    c. "I will never get over being hurt by my friend."

    d. "I wonder what it would be like if my husband were romantic like my friend's husband. Her husband is wonderful and so handsome ..."

    e. "He did that deliberately to embarrass me."

Chapter 10

The Attitudes of a Humble Heart

Webster's Dictionary defines an attitude as "a mental position with regard to a fact or state."[41] In other words, an attitude is what you think about an issue or about your circumstances. Attitudes can be good or bad. They can be sinful or godly. Whatever they are, they come from what you are thinking. The more your thoughts are biblical (if you are a Christian), the more pleasing your attitudes are to the Lord. The attitudes of a renewed mind are critical to godly living and flow out of pure, biblical thoughts. In the previous chapter we looked at biblical principles on right thinking. Now in this chapter and the next three chapters, we will see some of the attitudes that result from right thinking. In this chapter, we will cover the attitude of humility. In the next chapter, we will cover the attitudes of obedience, contentment, gratitude, servanthood, and forebearance. In the last two chapters of this section we will cover the attitudes of purity and love. Now let's begin with the attitude of humility.

The Attitude of Humility

What do the following people have in common?

A fifty-five year-old Bible study teacher is greatly offended when his new, much younger, pastor questions what he is teaching. He says to him, "Don't you trust me?"

A young wife and mother becomes instantly angry when her husband teases her. Everyone in the room tells her she is over-reacting.

The grandparent of a young woman in the church dies. She assumes that people in the church know but actually they do not. She does not say anything to anyone about the death, but her feelings are very hurt because no one in the church paid any attention to her in her loss.

An older man in the church reacts angrily to something his pastor said in his sermon. He doesn't even consider the possibility that he may be wrong and the pastor may be right or that he may have misunderstood what was said.

One of the women (an original member of the church) assumes that everyone wants the church run her way. She is especially pushy when it comes to decorating the new church building.

A young woman brags to anyone who will listen about how she is serving the Lord.

A woman critically condemns as unsaved or carnal those who do not adhere to her "rules" about makeup, movies, and dress.

Any wife and mother who puts herself first in her family.

A woman who becomes ill at church during a service and throws up. Everyone looks to see what has happened. She is so embarrassed she won't go back to church.

A wife who will not go to church unless her husband is with her. It bothers her what other people might think.

Any age Christian woman who refuses to listen to reproof. She cries and becomes angry and verbally attacks the person trying to help her. She says sarcastically, "I guess I can't do anything right!"

A man who believes that he deserves God's blessings and favor because of all that he has done for Him.

A young, beautiful woman who apologizes for how she looks to everyone who will listen.

A middle aged woman who still agonizes over how embarrassed she felt at her eighth birthday party when she tripped and dropped her cake and everyone laughed.

What do these people have in common? You probably have guessed. It is pride. Pride is manifested in many different ways. Since everyone does not display each and every way, it is very possible to see pride clearly in others, but not see it in ourselves. We may easily and gladly give God the credit for our gifts and abilities and yet verbally fight "to the death" to prove that we are right when others reprove us. Since pride is such a pervasive sin and God hates it, what is the cure? The cure is humility.

Humility is thinking no higher of yourself than you ought to think by viewing yourself and God through an accurate biblical perspective. Thus your focus is on pleasing and serving God and others, not on yourself. In order to understand the attitude of humility, we need to first consider what the Scripture teaches us.

Biblical Principles on Humility

1. We are not to think more highly of ourselves than we ought to think.

    For through the grace given to me I say to everyone among you not to think more highly of himself than he ought to think; but to think so as to have sound judgment, as God has allotted to each a measure of faith. **Romans 12:3**

It is ever so common for people to be *self*-centered instead of *God*-centered. In fact, everyone to some degree is self-centered. Some, if not most, are obsessed with thinking about themselves. Our culture practically screams in our ears, "Put **yourself** first. **You're** special. **You're** significant. **You** have worth. **You** must have your needs met. **Your** self-esteem is important. **You** have a right to feel a certain way!!" It is no wonder, then, that we easily think of ourselves first and foremost instead of thinking of God and others. It is also no wonder that those of us who are Christians can weave God very cleverly into our self-focus.

One way we weave God into our self-focus is by having a self-focused view of the universe. Being overly taken with our own importance, we try to obligate God to grant our wishes and make us feel special. God, however, does not have to obey us. He is God and we are His creatures, here to serve Him as He pleases. Instead of viewing ourselves as the center of the universe, our view of ourselves should be a biblically accurate one with right thinking about God and right thinking about ourselves as His creatures. With a biblically accurate view of ourselves, what we desire and think we need or want pales in comparison to the glory of God, our Maker. That is thinking rightly instead of thinking more highly of ourselves than we ought to think.

2. God gave us our gifts and abilities.

> *But by the grace of God I am what I am, and His grace toward me did not prove vain; but I labored even more than all of them, yet not I, but the grace of God with me.*
> *1 Corinthians 15:10*

It is easy for us to see God's amazing transforming grace in the life of the Apostle Paul. After all, Paul was guilty of hating and killing Christians. After God gave him a new heart, Paul's energies and passions were directed at glorifying God and telling everyone that "Jesus is Lord!" But what about us? It does not seem to me to be any less of a miracle of God's grace when He saved us. Before that, we were His enemies. Now we are at peace with God and have been given spiritual gifts by Him to serve Him. God has also given us natural abilities such as intelligence or artistic ability. Any and all of the abilities that we have (even if we had them before we became Christians) were given to us by God. A humble person remembers and affirms with the Apostle Paul that it is by God's grace that **"I am what I am"** (I Corinthians 15:10).

3. We are to give preference to others.

> *Be devoted to one another in brotherly love; give preference to one another in honor...* **Romans 12:10**

Children who are spoiled and indulged thrive on having their way. Children who are not spoiled and indulged also want their way, they just do not express it quite so strongly. Why would any child prefer himself? The reason is that children are born sinners and sinners are proud and naturally prefer self over others. Most adults do too. It may be easy for a Grandmother to make sacrifices for her precious little grandbaby, but how easy is it for her to prefer her husband's wishes over hers? Certainly no one is really exempt from preferring self instead of deferring as an honor to others.

One key to preferring (and deferring) to the other person is **"regarding one another as more important than yourselves..."** (Philippians 2:3). When you think of others in that light, it makes it easier to prefer their opinion because you see them as more important than you are. This attitude is a far cry from the spoiled child who angrily demands his way, but as the Apostle Paul wrote in Philippians 2:3, *that* is **"humility of mind..."**

4. The humble person is capable of learning God's ways.

> *He leads the humble in justice, and He teaches the humble His way.* **Psalm 25:9**

There is a dear old children's book written in the 1800's entitled *The Weed with An Ill Name*.[42] One of the main characters is a boy named George Franklin. George was wealthy and spoiled, and when he went to live with his Aunt and Uncle on their farm (because his father was sick), his selfishness and arrogance became very obvious. George was puffed up with his self-importance. He also was obnoxious and unpleasant to be around. George was unteachable and thus proud. He would not listen to adults nor to his sister and he certainly would not listen to God's Word (except where it benefited him to use it against others). God does not illumine His precious truths to those who are arrogant know-it-alls. It is only to the humble and contrite that God will even look. There was no fruit of the Spirit in George's life and it was not until much later that God saved him and gave him a humble heart. Then George became teachable, and only then was he capable of learning God's ways.

5. We are to put on a heart of humility.

> *So, as those who have been chosen of God, holy and be-loved, <u>put on a heart</u> of compassion, kindness, <u>humility,</u> gentleness and patience; bearing with one another, and forgiving each other, whoever has a complaint against anyone; just as the Lord forgave you, so also should you.*
> *Colossians 3:12, emphasis added*

For part of my childhood we lived in Washington, D.C. In the winter it would sometimes snow, and of course I wanted to go outside and play in the snow. My mother would say, "Put on your snowsuit, boots, gloves, and hat!" So the process would begin. It probably took a good ten minutes to put on all that paraphernalia and out I would go. It was probably less than ten minutes later when I would come in, wet and cold, and take it all off. This put on and put off process would continue throughout the day until my mother had enough of it and made me stay indoors. It took work on my mother's part to put on my boots and snowsuit just as it takes work on our part to put on humility. In fact, putting on humility is a much harder feat than putting on a snowsuit. Unfortunately because of our tendency to sin humility is much easier to take off and leave behind than a dripping wet snowsuit.

Putting on humility takes work. It takes the work of God to enable us. It takes work on our part to think and respond in a humble manner. God will always graciously do His part. Our part is to obey His command daily to **"put on a heart of ... humility"** (Colossians 3:12).

6. The more humble we are, the more we please God and will be rewarded by Him.

> *...and all of you, <u>clothe yourselves with humility</u> toward one another, for GOD IS OPPOSED TO THE PROUD, BUT GIVES GRACE TO THE HUMBLE. <u>Therefore humble yourselves under the mighty hand of God, that He may exalt you at the proper time</u>, casting all your anxiety on Him, because He cares for you.*   *1 Peter 5:5-7, emphasis added*

Rewards are always great. Prisoners are released from prison early as a reward for good behavior. Children learn the habit of making up their bed or brushing their teeth by the reward of gold stars on a chart. There are rewards for people who are faithful on a diet, usually some sort of low fat or low sugar dessert. Some employers give bonuses for jobs well done. I have told each of our grandchildren that I will (Lord willing, if I live long enough) give them one hundred dollars when they turn twenty-one if they have never smoked or taken a puff of a cigarette. God created all of us to enjoy rewards and He promises rewards that make a grandmother's reward to her grandchildren pale in comparison.

God promises to exalt us, but only as we please Him by humbling ourselves. How and when God exalts us is up to Him, but like the employee who receives an unexpected bonus, it will bring us joy. Our joy will be magnified as we realize that He has rewarded us for the humility that He has given us. Thus He receives all the glory. We humble ourselves by discerning when we are proud, turning from our sin, and consequently thinking and acting in a humble manner. Then we will have **"clothed ourselves with humility"** (1 Peter 5:6). Then, **"He may exalt you at the proper time"** (1 Peter 5:6).

7. God dwells with the humble.

> *For thus says the high and exalted One who lives forever, whose name is Holy, "I dwell on a high and holy place and also with the contrite and lowly of spirit in order to revive the spirit of the lowly and to revive the heart of the contrite."*   *Isaiah 57:15*

Contrary to what some people might think, God does not *dwell* everywhere. Certainly, He is all-knowing, all-seeing, and everything is in God's presence, but He is not a "force" dwelling within the trees and there is not a little spark of Him in each person which will grow and grow until they become one with God and the universe. He is selective with whom He dwells. God spoke to the prophet

Isaiah and then Isaiah, in turn, told the people what God had revealed to him. Isaiah had seen God in His **"high and holy place"** and described the experience this way, **"I saw the Lord sitting on a throne, lofty and exalted, with the train of His robe filling the temple"** (Isaiah 6:1). God also let Isaiah see his sin which caused him to mourn over being a **"man of unclean lips"** (Isaiah 6:5). God gave Isaiah a contrite heart and lowly spirit (the ability to see his sin and grieve over it). The Lord Jesus taught us, **"Blessed are the poor in spirit, for theirs is the kingdom of heaven. Blessed are those who mourn, for they shall be comforted"** (Matthew 5:3-4). Proud people are puffed up. They do not see their desperate need for God. God in His kindness and mercy gives some the blessing of seeing their sin for what it is. Those are the people with whom God dwells.

8. God gives grace (favor, undeserved blessings) to the humble.

> *But He gives a greater grace. Therefore it says, "GOD IS OPPOSED TO THE PROUD, BUT GIVES GRACE TO THE HUMBLE."*   *James 4:6*

You probably have heard it said or you may have said it yourself, "When I was a teenager I did not think my parents knew anything. Now that I am an adult, I see wisdom in what they were trying to tell me." Why would any teenager not see wisdom in what their parents are trying to tell him? Because they are proud and arrogant. A proud person won't listen; they "know it all." They are very exasperating to the person who is trying to reason with them. The more you try to help them, the more hysterical, theatrical, and determined they become to have their way. They have problems with their parents, co-workers, bosses, teachers, and friends. They have problems because they *are* a problem – sinfully proud and proud of it! They create strife and people oppose them. People are not the only ones who oppose them. God does too.

When God opposes someone (as He does the proud), He sets Himself against that person. He is not merely neutral or passive towards them but is actively opposing them, facing Himself against them. Being actively opposed by God is an extremely precarious and unnecessary place to be. God hates pride. It is an abomination to Him (Proverbs 6:16-17). It would be like running into a brick wall that not only stops your progress but is surrounding you, making it impossible for you to get around it. It is as futile as Balaam beating his donkey and demanding the donkey move on when all the while the Angel of the Lord was blocking his path (Numbers 22). Even though Balaam could not, at first, see God and we cannot see Him either, He is none-the-less there – opposing us when we are proud.

It is utterly crucial to realize that no one stops being proud until they start being humble and it goes without saying that no one was ever truly righteously humble apart from God's enabling grace. God gives grace to those who seek His help, who realize they don't "know it all." God's grace is His favor and help. We don't deserve it and we can't earn it, but we benefit from it as He enables us to obey Him and honor Him in our thoughts and actions.

When you are proud, God sets Himself against you. When you are humble, God gives you His grace. How then does a person with a humble attitude think and act?

Attitudes of Humility

1. You are aware of your need for God's grace and ask Him for humility.

   > *Therefore, since we have a great high priest who has passed through the heavens, Jesus the Son of God, let us hold fast our confession. For we do not have a high priest who cannot sympathize with our weaknesses, but One who has been tempted in all things as we are, yet without sin. Let us therefore draw near with confidence to the throne of grace, so that we may receive mercy and find grace to help in time of need.* **Hebrews 4:14-16**

   Humility does not come naturally to sinners, therefore we need supernatural help that can only come from God. Pray often for humility. As you go through your day, wherever you are and whatever you are doing, talk to the Lord Jesus (aloud or in your mind). Each time you are tempted to think or respond in pride, simply ask Him for mercy and His grace to help you. Tell Him, "Lord, this is one of my times of need."

2. You immediately think, "God show me where I'm wrong," instead of thinking, "I'm right and I will prove it."

   > *Humble yourselves in the presence of the Lord, and He will exalt you.* **James 4:10**

   Suppose you could construct a scale that measures how humbly you react to being told you are wrong. And suppose that scale ranged from zero to one hundred. Zero means you do not react in sinful pride at all and are only concerned about showing love to God and the other person. Zero would mean your very first thought is something like this, "Lord, how can I give you glory in this circumstance?" or "Lord, I think they are wrong about me, but if they are right, help me to understand. If they are, in fact, wrong, help me not to try to vindicate myself but only clarify the matter in such a way as to help them understand."

On the other extreme of the scale, one hundred means you become angry, feel frustrated, demand vindication, and passionately try to get everyone who will listen over on your side. You may have trouble sleeping because you could not stop thinking about what happened and how you felt. Your thoughts of the other person spiral down to wishing them ill-will – "perhaps they'll die or be hurt in some way." Your thoughts of God are blasphemous – "Why did God allow them to embarrass me like that?" You conclude, "I can't take it any more! I will never go back to that church again," or "I will never speak to that person again."

Most of us are not up to one hundred, although some are! Not one of us is at zero either if we are honest. We all fall somewhere in between. If you want to truly honor God, you must cultivate discernment (What kind of things are likely to cause me to react in pride?) and think a God-honoring, humble thought ("Lord, whether they ever perceive me rightly or not, use me for Your glory.").

3.   You have the attitude of "teach me," not "I know all I need to know."

> *Teach me, O LORD, the way of Your statutes, and I shall*
> *observe it to the end. Give me understanding, that I may*
> *observe Your law and keep it with all my heart.*
> ### Psalm 119:33-34

Have you ever tried to teach somebody something only to have them tersely say, "I know, I know!" and then proceed to do it wrong? It is very difficult to teach someone something if they are proud and will not listen. Once a friend of my husband's and mine called me because he knew I was a nurse and he was experiencing chest pain. The more I learned of his symptoms, the more concerned I became. It sounded very much like he was having a heart attack. His doctor and hospital were more than an hour's drive from him. I calmly but firmly told him he needed to call 911 and let the ambulance take him to the hospital. He refused and ended up calling another friend to drive him to the hospital. As he walked into the emergency room, he collapsed having a bad heart attack. In spite of the fact that he had no medical training and I did, he would not listen and assumed that he knew what was best for himself concerning his particular situation. Proud people are not teachable. They won't listen to someone who knows more about a subject than they do, and even more tragically, they won't listen to God either.

The humble man, on the other hand, has the attitude of the Psalmist who begged God to teach him and give him understanding. I suspect that no matter how much he came to understand and obey God's Word, he longed for greater understanding. This Psalmist humbled himself before God and, unlike my friend who would not listen, he listened and was teachable.

4. You think first of others' feelings and needs, not "What about me?"

> *Do nothing from selfishness or empty conceit, but with humility of mind regard one another as more important than yourselves; do not merely look out for your own personal interests, but also for the interests of others.*
> *Philippians 2:3-4*

I recently saw part of a television program in which a man was shot and probably would not live. When his wife arrived at the emergency room she was allowed to go into the room and talk to him. She was crying and said to him, "Don't do this to **me**! You can't leave **me**! I couldn't stand it if you died! What would **I** do?" She was understandably upset, but her focus was on herself instead of her poor husband who was dying. Her focus was so much on herself that I hoped that he could not hear her. She was looking out for herself instead of seeing him as **"more important than [her]self"** (Philippians 2:3-4, adaptation added).

All of us are selfish to one degree or another. We naturally think of ourselves first and not others. We think or say things like this:

How could she have done that to *me*?

That hurt *my* feelings.

I need *my* space.

I wish he would pay attention to *me*.

I want to go first.

I don't want to take a meal to her, she never does anything for me.

I'm not going to stay in the nursery. *I* hate the nursery. *I'd* rather be in church.

If I feel uncomfortable, *I'm* not going back.

He should make *me* feel special.

All of the above thoughts have one thing in common, they are self-focused. Instead of being puffed up with our own importance, we should be thinking of God's glory and thinking of people as more important than we are. For example, "He should make me feel special" should be "What can I do to make him feel special, whether he responds or not?" Another example is "I'm not going to stay in the nursery. I hate the nursery. I'd rather be in church." Rather than being selfish about serving, a right thought would be, "I'd rather not stay in the nursery (who would?). But I want the young parents to have a break and be able to hear the sermon. I can listen to the tape later."

A humble person thinks first of others, not themselves. They are not like the wife in the emergency room who was thinking only of herself. They consider the other person as more important.

5. You give God the credit for your achievements and salvation. You do not think, "Look what I have done!"

> *Thus says the LORD, "Let not a wise man boast of his wisdom, and let not a mighty man boast of his might, let not a rich man boast of his riches; but let him who boasts boast of this, that he understands and knows Me, that I am the LORD who exercises lovingkindness, justice and righteousness on earth; for I delight in these things," declares the LORD.*   *Jeremiah 9:23-24*

Some people are braggarts! They brag about their education, how hard they worked in school, their job, how successful they are at work, how much money they make, and how they deserve so much more than those with lesser jobs. They may smugly say or think, "Look how hard I've worked and what I have achieved."

People who are braggarts frighten me because they leave God completely out of their bragging. They may be very well-educated, successful, and wealthy, but they are to be pitied in comparison to the humble man. The humble man may have had to struggle to graduate from high school, may have to work an extra part-time job to make ends meet, may have a tedious job that is boring and hard labor, and may have a hard life. Yet the humble man is grateful to the Lord for what abilities and material things he has. The humble man (whether rich or poor) boasts in what the Lord has done and in His goodness, not in what he believes he has personally accomplished. God delights in him.

6. You are truly worshiping God, not merely going through the motions of religious pretense.

> *[Jesus said,] "Two <u>men went up into the temple to pray,</u> one a Pharisee and the other a tax collector. The Pharisee*

stood and was praying this to himself: 'God, I thank You that I am not like other people: swindlers, unjust, adulterers, or even like this tax collector. I fast twice a week; I pay tithes of all that I get.' But the tax collector, standing some distance away, was even unwilling to lift up his eyes to heaven, but was beating his breast, saying, 'God, be merciful to me, the sinner! I tell you, this man went to his house justified rather than the other; for everyone who exalts himself will be humbled, but he who humbles himself will be exalted."

Luke 18:10-14, emphasis added

Recently I heard our pastor, John Crotts, talk about the Christmas Eve service at our church this past year. He said that during communion and while the congregation was singing, he was thinking about the Lord Jesus in heaven listening to our praise and worship of Him. He imagined what worship would be like in the presence of the Lord.

John could have been thinking, "I wonder what they thought of my sermon?" or "How does my new shirt and tie look?" or "I wonder if those visitors liked me?" or "I am so glad that I am not like some of the people in our church. They've done some horrible things." Instead of being focused on how wonderful he believed himself to be, John's focus was on worshiping God. He was not like the Pharisee who went to the temple to show off. He was more like the humble man who saw his sin and asked for mercy. He was worshiping God, not merely going through the motions of religious pretense.

7. You are willing to suffer humiliation and embarrassment for Jesus' sake even if you are never vindicated in this life.

If you are reviled for the name of Christ, you are blessed, because the Spirit of glory and of God rests on you. Make sure that none of you suffers as a murderer, or thief, or evildoer, or a troublesome meddler, but if anyone suffers as a Christian, he is not to be ashamed, but is to glorify God in this name...Therefore, those who suffer according to the will of God shall entrust their souls to a faithful Creator in doing what is right. 1 Peter 4:14-16,19

As a Christian, I have confronted others with their sin or presented the gospel to them. Many more times than not, the person receiving the reproof responds in a God-honoring way; but if they come under conviction and are not humble, they become upset with me. Because of their sinful pride, they may perceive that my motive was to embarrass them. They may think, "She thinks she's better than I am," or "she deliberately hurt my feelings," or "she's not compassionate." Even though I only wanted to help them and in spite of the fact that Proverbs 27:6 says that **"faithful are the wounds of a friend,"** they felt hurt and angry. If they do not repent of their pride, they will likely pull away from me and may talk about me to others in a negative way. Sometimes their "talk" gets back to me.

It may not be difficult if someone you barely know never says, "I was wrong about you and I slandered you. Will you forgive me?" But it can break your heart when the person is your dearest, best friend and she thinks you have lost your mind! It is during these painful times, however, that we are to humble ourselves, give God glory, count ourselves blessed by God, and trust that we are **"suffer[ing] according to the will of God"** (1 Peter 4:19, adaptation added), even if we are never vindicated in this life!

Conclusion

Earlier in this chapter we learned that humility is thinking no higher of yourself than you ought to think by viewing yourself and God through an accurate biblical perspective. We saw that our responsibility is (by God's grace) to put on a heart of humility. What about you? Where are you on a scale that measures pride and humility? Is God helping you or opposing you? Nothing else will be right and none of your other attitudes will be pleasing to God if you are proud and unteachable. Is your attitude consistently, "Show me Lord," "Help me Lord," and "Use me Lord even if I must have my feelings hurt and suffer embarrassment." How does God view you? Are you humble or are you proud? What is your prayer?

Chapter 10

Study Questions

1. From the second paragraph on page 147, define humility.

2. If you have a biblically accurate view of yourself, whom is your focus on?

3. From reading 1 Corinthians 15:10, what was the Apostle Paul's attitude about the incredible gifts that he had?

4. A humble person prefers others over themselves. Where in the Bible does it tell us to **"regard one another as more important than yourselves..."**? Give a personal example of how you could prefer others.

5. Have you ever tried to teach someone who was arrogant and disagreed with you, yet you know you were right? That is how we respond to God sometimes. According to Psalm 25:9, who is it that God will teach?

6. What do you learn from Colossians 3:12 about the issue of your humility and your responsibility?

7. What sort of reward might you expect if you humble yourself before God? See 1 Peter 5:5-7.

8. What does it mean to have a contrite heart and lowly spirit? See Isaiah 57:15.

9. What happens when God opposes someone? See principle # 8 on page 151.

10. Correct the following proud thoughts with a humble thought:
    a. "I don't care what they say, I know I'm right!"

    b. "I can handle this."

    c. "Why did God allow them to embarrass me like that?"

d. While listening to someone reprove you, you think, "I know, I know, I wish they would hurry up!"

e. "That hurt my feelings. I'll show her what it's like."

f. "If I feel uncomfortable, I'm not going back."

g. "He should make me feel special."

h. "I've really worked hard at this job. I deserve this raise."

i. "Next week I'm going to go on vacation and no one is going to stop me."

j. "God, thank You that I am better than these other people."

Chapter 11

The Attitudes of
A Godly Heart

Our daughter Anna has a new dog. The dog's name is Daisy. I am not sure what kind of dog Daisy is, but it does appear she will be large based on the size of her paws. Daisy is a very enthusiastic puppy and not very well trained. It is obvious that she is consumed with herself — playing, digging large holes in the yard, eating, etc. Consequently, Daisy is frequently in trouble. Anna and Tony and the children are using dog "behavior modification" techniques to train Daisy. Frankly, I have not seen much progress, but Tony assures me these things take time.

Daisy is not very *obedient*, certainly not *content* to sit quietly out of the way and entertain herself, although she does appear, at times, to be *grateful*, especially for her food. Daisy hasn't a clue about waiting patiently with *forbearance*. Instead of being a *servant* to others, she creates "servant" opportunities for others to clean up her messes! Since Daisy is a dog, Anna and Tony don't expect much but they keep trying. The children, on the other hand, are a different story. Anna and Tony should and do expect Tommy, Kelsey, and Jordan to be obedient, content, servants, grateful, and forbearing. (Concerning the children, I have seen a lot of progress but, as with Daisy, these things take time)!

The lessons Daisy has to learn will probably only take a short time. Otherwise we will have seen the last of Daisy. Concerning the children, however, by God's grace they will be making progress in all of the godly heart's attitudes for the rest of their lives. It is not only Anna's and Tony's desire that the children mature in these attitudes, but it is God's desire also; and like the children, all of us need to mature in these areas.

The Attitude of Obedience

A Christian with an *obedient heart has a desire to and strives to perfectly keep the commandments of God.* Obviously, no human being can perfectly obey God but with God's help Christians should be improving (1 John 1:8-10). Not only should their outward actions be improving but also their motives (desires) should grow more and more to want to please the Lord. Obedience is more than simple outward behavior as we will see from the following biblical principles.

Biblical Principles Concerning the Attitude of Obedience

1. The Lord Jesus Christ is our example. *Have this attitude in yourselves which was also in Christ Jesus, who, although He existed in the form of God, did not regard equality with God a thing to be grasped, but emptied Himself, taking the form of a bond-servant, and being made in the likeness of men. And being found in appearance as a man, He humbled Himself by <u>becoming obedient to the point of death</u>, even death on a cross.* **Philippians 2:5-8, emphasis added**
2. An obedient person puts God's desires ahead of their own desires. *And He went a little beyond them, and fell on His face and prayed, saying, "My Father, if it is possible, let this cup pass from Me; <u>yet not as I will, but as You will</u>."* **Matthew 26:39, emphasis added**
3. We are to behave in a godly manner. *<u>As obedient children</u>, do not be conformed to the former lusts which were yours in your ignorance, but like the Holy One who called you, be holy yourselves also in all your behavior; because it is written, "YOU SHALL BE HOLY, FOR I AM HOLY."* **1 Peter 1:14-16, emphasis added**

4. We are to obey God even if we must suffer for it.

The high priest questioned them [Peter and the apostles], saying, "We gave you strict orders not to continue teaching in this name, and behold, you have filled Jerusalem with your teaching and intend to bring this man's blood upon us." But Peter and the apostles answered and said, "We must obey God rather than men..."
Acts 5:27-29, adaptation and emphasis added

5. Obedience is an evidence of salvation.

By this we know that we have come to know Him, if we keep His commandments. The one who says, "I have come to know Him," and does not keep His commandments, is a liar, and the truth is not in Him; but whoever keeps His word, in him the love of God has truly been perfected.
1 John 2:3-5, emphasis added

6. Obedience is living by faith (knowing God and trusting that He knows what is best for you), not by sight.

By faith Abraham, when he was called, obeyed by going out to a place which he was to receive for an inheritance; and he went out, not knowing where he was going.
Hebrews 11:8, emphasis added

7. Those who obey God are those who love the Lord.

[Jesus said to the Disciples], "If you love Me, you will keep My commandments."   John 14:15

8. To those who love the Lord, His commands are not burdensome.

For this is the love of God, that we keep His commandments; and His commandments are not burdensome.
1 John 5:3, emphasis added

God expects obedience. He wants to be first in our life, not last. As we obey, He molds us into His character. Obedience is by faith because we trust God that He will be with us and know what is best for us. Obedience is a test of our love for Him and because it is for Him, it is not a burden. Now that we have seen these biblical principles, let's turn our attention to application of those principles.

Practical Ways to have an Obedient Heart

1. A person with an obedient heart can sing hymns such as *Oh, How I Love Jesus* and it is a true statement.

   > Are you playing church? Do you merely go through the ceremony by rote? Are the words you sing simply vain repetition or do you sincerely think about what you are singing? When you sing the hymn, *Oh, How I Love Jesus,* is it true because you are obeying the Lord?

2. A person with an obedient heart is obedient whether they want to be or not.

   > Do you greet others with kindness even if you are having a bad day? Do you do what is right for Jesus' sake even if you are aggravated with another person? Do you graciously obey the authorities over you when you would prefer to be doing something else?

3. A person with an obedient heart lives their life based on the Word of God and not their feelings.

   > What is the ruling factor in your life, Scripture or how you feel? Do you tend to lean **"on your own understanding"** (Proverbs 3:5-6) or do you trust God and His Word? Do you ever embarrass yourself because you know you reacted emotionally and greatly overreacted?

4. A person with an obedient heart is willing to stand up to peer pressure.

   > Are you discerning about the wrong influences others have on you? Wrong influences may result in gossip, worry, or bitterness toward your husband. Will you, in love, try to help them with their sin?

5. A person with an obedient heart is not walking with the rest of the world, they are different.

    Is your life different because you are not like the world? Do you unnecessarily offend people or does your life draw others to the Lord and convict those living in sin?

6. A person with an obedient heart has joy in doing what God wants. It is not a chore for them.

    Are you delighted to be able to please God and serve Him? What about in the difficult times of your life? Do you dread obeying God or do you anticipate it with joy?

Summary of the Attitude of Obedience

This section began with and is ending with the Lord Jesus Christ. He is our example and He was obedient to the point of death. He also was perfectly obedient throughout His entire life on earth. He was not walking as the rest of the world but was walking perfectly with His Father in heaven. If we truly love Him, we will do what He has told us in His Word and it will be our joy.

The Attitude of a Contented Heart

Abraham was one hundred and seventy-five years old when he died and Scripture tells us that he **"breathed his last and died in a ripe old age, an old man and satisfied with life; and he was gathered to his people"** (Genesis 25:8). What a way to go! — with peace of mind, having lived most of what we know of his life in obedience to the Lord. Then when death was near, Abraham was content to leave this world behind and go into eternity with his Lord.

Death is probably the most extreme circumstance that one has to individually endure yet Abraham was content. His contentment certainly did not come from the trials of extreme age nor from his impending death. He had a contented heart not because of outward circumstances but because of what he thought about them. Thinking of Abraham as our example, the attitude of a contented heart can be defined as follows:

> *Contentment is an inward grace given by God that results in a mindset of being satisfied to stay in your circumstances for as long as God wills.*

Abraham's satisfaction and contentment were rooted in God just as ours should be. In order to learn more about godly contentment, let's see what the Scriptures teach us.

Biblical Principles on Contentment

1. We can learn to be content no matter how tough things are because God will help us.

   Not that I speak from want, for <u>I have learned to be content</u> in whatever circumstances I am....<u>I can do all things through Him who strengthens me</u>.
   Philippians 4:11-13, emphasis added

2. We are to be content with the necessities of life.

   If we have food and covering, with these we shall be content.   *1 Timothy 6:8*

3. Be content with what you have today. Focus on seeking God and pleasing Him.

   "For this reason I say to you, do not be anxious about your life, as to what you shall eat or what you shall drink; nor for your body, as to what you shall put on. Is not life more than food, and the body than clothing?... <u>But seek first His kingdom and His righteousness, and all these things will be added to you</u>."
   Matthew 6:25,33, emphasis added

4. A person who is content does not complain.

   "Nor let us try the Lord, as some of them did, and were destroyed by the serpents. Nor grumble, as some of them did, and were destroyed by the destroyer."
   1 Corinthians 10:9-10 (see also Philippians 2:14-16)

5. True contentment means we do not have to sin against God.

> *Then Job arose and tore his robe and shaved his head, and he fell to the ground and worshiped. He said, "Naked I came from my mother's womb, and naked I shall return there. The LORD gave and the LORD has taken away. Blessed be the name of the LORD." Through all this Job did not sin nor did he blame God.*　　　*Job 1:20-22*

> *"But it is still my consolation. And I rejoice in unsparing pain, that I have not denied the words of the Holy One."*
> *Job 6:10*

Practical Ways to have a Contented Heart

1. True contentment can only come from God. The natural heart is lustful after *more,* whether it is sex, excitement, money, or security. It can never be satisfied.

   Do you go shopping and purchase items you do not need or can not afford because it makes you feel better? Are you satisfied with what God has provided for you? Does it make you unhappy when you cannot have what other's have?

2. Contentment comes from being in a right standing with God.

   Is contentment and satisfaction in the Lord eluding you? Is pleasing God your greatest desire? When you read the Scriptures, does it give you hope and quiet you? Are you sure that you are in right standing with God?

3. Contentment is a mindset. It's not what you have that makes you content, it's what you tell yourself about it.

   Are you more likely to think, "I want" or "I need" than you are to think, "If the Lord wills?" When you do not have your way, is your attitude "God is the only one who can know if my circumstances being different would give Him glory."

4.   It is a sin not to be content with what the Lord has given you.

> Are you a complainer? For some people nothing is ever right. Are you one of those? Are you more likely to complain or to thank God for trying circumstances?

Summary of the Attitude of a Contented Heart

Being content does not depend on what you do or do not possess but what you tell yourself about your possessions. Contentment results from knowing and trusting God. It is a grace gift from God to the Christian regardless of the Christian's outward circumstances. A person with the heart's attitude of contentment is like Abraham — he trusts God and is willing to wait, content to rest in God's promises.

The Attitude of a Servant's Heart

The ultimate servant, the servant above all other servants, is our Lord Jesus Christ. He was the servant who did not have to be a servant. After all, He was God yet He humbled Himself by becoming a man. In the process, though, He suffered greatly. According to the book of Isaiah **"His appearance was marred more than any man..."** and **"He was despised and forsaken of men, a man of sorrows, and acquainted with grief..."** **"He was oppressed and He was afflicted, yet He did not open His mouth..."** and the supreme example of His being a servant for others occurred as **"He poured out Himself to death..."** as He **"bore the sin of many, and interceded for the transgressors"** (Isaiah 52:14, 53:3, 7, 12).

Christ's agony on the cross was for a brief time and then it was finished. He is now receiving the esteem and adoration that He deserves. As we go about our daily lives, all the saints and angels in heaven are praising and worshiping Him. Seven hundred years before the Lord Jesus came to earth as a man, God prophesied of a future day when **"Behold My servant will prosper, He will be high and lifted up, and greatly exalted"** (Isaiah 52:13).

Just as the Lord Jesus Christ became a servant for us, we are in turn to become a servant for Him. So *a person with a servant's heart is someone who has the desire to be a voluntary servant to the Lord Jesus Christ and it shows in their actions and attitudes.* Let's turn our attention to some of the biblical principles concerning being a servant.

Biblical Principles on the Attitude of a Servant's Heart

1. The Apostle Paul saw himself as a bond-servant to the Lord Jesus Christ.   *Paul, a bond-servant of Christ Jesus, called as an apostle, set apart for the gospel of God, which He promised beforehand through His prophets in the Holy Scriptures, concerning His Son...*   *Romans 1:1-3, emphasis added*
2. God will reward those with a servant's heart.   *But Jesus called them to Himself, and said, "You know that the rulers of the Gentiles lord it over them, and their great men exercise authority over them. It is not so among you, but whoever wishes to become great among you shall be your servant, and whoever wishes to be first among you shall be your slave; just as the Son of Man did not come to be served, but to serve and to give His life a ransom for many."*   *Matthew 20:25-28, emphasis added*
3. The mark of a true servant is his faithfulness.   *"Who then is the faithful and sensible slave whom his master put in charge of his household to give them their food at the proper time? Blessed is that slave whom his master finds so doing when he comes."*   *Matthew 24:45-46, emphasis added*
4. As a servant of the Lord Jesus, we should be servants to others.   *...just as you learned it from Epaphras, our beloved fellow bond-servant, who is a faithful servant of Christ on our behalf, and he also informed us of your love in the Spirit.*   *Colossians 1:7-8, emphasis added*

5. A servant is not greater than his master. So, there will be times you will suffer persecution if you are truly the Lord Jesus' servant.

   Jesus said, "Remember the word that I said to you, 'A slave is not greater than his master.' <u>If they persecuted Me, they will also persecute you</u>; if they kept My word, they will keep yours also."'
   John 15:20, emphasis added

6. We are not to be slaves to men.

   You were bought with a price; do not become slaves of men.   *1 Corinthians 7:23*

7. We choose to become a servant.

   Have this attitude in yourselves which was also in Christ Jesus, who, although He existed in the form of God, <u>did not regard equality with God a thing to be grasped</u>, but emptied Himself, taking the form of a bond-servant, and being made in the likeness of men.
   Philippians 2:5-7, emphasis added

8. Some of the characteristics that the Lord's bondservant must strive for are to not be quarrelsome and *to* be kind, able to teach, patient when wronged, gently correcting those in opposition.

   <u>And the Lord's bond-servant must not be</u> quarrelsome, but be kind to all, able to teach, patient when wronged, with gentleness correcting those who are in opposition, if perhaps God may grant them repentance leading to the knowledge of the truth, and they may come to their senses and escape from the snare of the devil, having been held captive by him to do his will.
   2 Timothy 2:24-26, emphasis added

Summary of Principles

The Apostle Paul called himself a bond-servant of Christ. Pastors and elders are the Lord's bond-servants and we, likewise, are to be His bond-servants. Servants follow the example of their Master and they are faithful whether others are watching or not. There are rewards for faithful servants who may, in this life, suffer persecution. Now that we have seen some of the biblical principles on being a servant, let's turn our attention to practical application.

Practical Ways to have a Servant's Heart

1. Our chores take on a new purpose when we do them as a servant to the Lord.

   Do you resent that pile of dirty clothes and mound of ironing or do you talk and sing to the Lord as you do your work? As you do your chores, do you consider that you are doing them for the Lord and He is looking at your heart?

2. God wants us to be faithful day-by-day, not just have occasional periodic bursts of enthusiasm.

   Can you be depended on to keep the nursery at church and be on time *and* have a good attitude? Is your life characterized by being a faithful servant to the Lord and others whether you are in the mood or not? (See 1 Corinthians 4:2.)

3. We are to be faithful to be kind and gentle with others.

   Is your first reaction to another's sin, a sharp, sarcastic tone of voice or do you think, "Lord, how can I help them?" What about at home with your family? Do you speak kind and gentle words or do you treat them according to however you happen to feel at the moment?

4. Ask God to give you a servant's heart that He will use for His glory.

   When your day is unexpectedly interrupted by an elderly relative who needs help, do you pray and ask God to give you a servant's heart or do you sigh in frustration? Do you desire to be more godly and to serve others, but struggle with resentment when it comes to your own family?

5. Look for things you can do for others.

   Do you think about and seek ways to help others or are you lazy and selfish and look for ways to get out of doing good deeds for others? Do you only desire to serve if others are around to notice or are you content to serve whether anyone finds out or not? Do you only serve your family or do you reach outside of your family and help others?

6. Like Joshua, decide now whom you are going to serve. (See Joshua 24:15.)

7. Is it God you are serving by being obedient to His Word or is it your worldly pleasures and self interests? Have you already made up your mind that you will serve God even if you are tempted to do otherwise?

Summary of a Servant's Heart

True servants of God gladly see themselves as a bond-servant to their one and only Master, the Lord Jesus Christ. They are faithful as the greatest servant of all was faithful. They are not slaves to mere men and have already made up their minds whom they will serve. Because they are servant's to the Lord, they are also servants to others. Their attitude is one of humble servanthood and not resentment as they seek ways to help others. Their desire to serve others is God-given and it is shown in their faithful, good works.

Attitude of a Grateful Heart

We have a new grandbaby, Carter Lawson Peace, born yesterday afternoon. He is number seven for us but every bit as precious as numbers one through six. You can imagine the scene in the hall at the hospital when our son, David, came to the waiting room to get us and said, "Come and see the baby." There were grandparents, brothers, one uncle and his date, and friends. We crowded around the tiny baby's bassinet. Everyone was exclaiming how beautiful he was and how perfect. People who did not know us were smiling as they walked by.

A little later in the evening after our daughter-in-law, Jaimee, was settled into her room, the nurse brought Carter to her. Well, we piled into the room to get an even closer look. Flashes from cameras were going off and we took turns holding him. As I took him in my arms, I looked at him and said, "Carter, this is Grandmama. I love you very much." My eyes filled with tears and my heart filled with *gratitude* to the Lord for this child.

It is not too difficult to be grateful for a new, precious baby. But what about expressing gratitude to God for a difficult trial? Scripture is very clear that we are to be thankful for all things, good or bad. This attitude may seem impossible yet it has to be possible for a child of God to obey Him. First, let's consider some biblical principles on the attitude of a grateful heart and then we will look at several practical examples.

Someone who is not grateful to God must be the ultimate ingrate. Some people are never happy, never satisfied, and never grateful. They grumble and complain *to* others and *about* others. Because of their sinful pride, they also grumble and complain *to* God and *about* God. They are like a whiney, spoiled child who wants more. Not being thankful becomes a way of life, a sinful habit. Whereas the ingrate always finds something to complain about, *the Christian with a grateful heart is thankful to God in all things whether their circumstances are good or bad.* Let's begin this section by looking at some of the Scriptures that pertain to gratitude.

Biblical Principles on the Attitude of a Grateful Heart

1. We are to be thankful for God's gift of grace to us, the Lord Jesus Christ. *Thanks be to God for His indescribable gift!* **2 Corinthians 9:15**
2. Gratefulness to God is part of worshiping Him. *Shout joyfully to the LORD, all the earth. Serve the LORD with gladness; Come before Him with joyful singing. Know that the LORD Himself is God; It is He who has made us, and not we ourselves; We are His people and the sheep of His pasture. Enter His gates with thanksgiving and His courts with praise. Give thanks to Him, bless His name. For the LORD is good; His lovingkindness is everlasting and His faithfulness to all generations.* **Psalm 100:1-5**

3. Not being grateful to God is a characteristic of unbelievers.

   For even though they knew God, they did not honor Him as God or give thanks, but they became futile in their speculations, and their foolish heart was darkened.
   Romans 1:21

4. We are commanded to be thankful.

   Let the peace of Christ rule in your hearts, to which indeed you were called in one body; and be thankful.
   Colossians 3:15

5. Be thankful for whatever God brings your way.

   ...in everything give thanks; for this is God's will for you in Christ Jesus. *1 Thessalonians 5:18*

   He [Job] said, "Naked I came from my mother's womb, and naked I shall return there. The LORD gave and the LORD has taken away. Blessed be the name of the LORD." *Job 1:21 (Explanation added)*

Summary of the Biblical Principles
on the Attitude of a Grateful Heart

Gratefulness to God is a vital part of worship of Him. We, like the singers of Israel, should sing His praises with thanksgiving. We should also never tire of thanking Him for His indescribable grace gift to us, the Lord Jesus Christ. It is typical of unbelievers to be ungrateful to God because sin has darkened their understanding, but it is typical of believers to stay in a habitual state of being thankful. Their gratitude is irrespective of their circumstances. Now that we have considered some of the biblical principles on the attitude of a grateful heart, let's turn our attention to practical application in our own life.

Practical Ways to have a Heart of Gratitude

1. A thankful person sees the grace of God in their trials.

    Do you see tests and trials as filtered through the hands of your loving heavenly Father or do you become angry because things do not go your way? When faced with a trial, is this how *you* might think? – "God *thank You* for this test and what You are wanting to teach me and others." Or "Lord *thank You* that I will not have to live in this sin-cursed body or world forever." Or *"Thank You* Lord Jesus for reminding me how much I need You." Or *"Thank You* for this opportunity to give you glory." Or "Lord, *thank You* that I do not have to go through this trial in vain, that you have a purpose in it for me — to give You glory by conforming me more and more to Your image." Or *"Thank You* for loving me so much that You allowed me the privilege of having my faith tested at this level."

2. A thankful person does not become bitter or angry with God when adversity comes.

    Are you convinced of God's goodness? Are you glad for His sovereign care over you? When a trial comes upon you, do you run to God for comfort and help or do you shake your fist at Him and cry out in anger?

3. Instead of being sinfully disappointed, a thankful person gives their expectations to God and waits to see how God decides to work.

    Do you set your heart so much on circumstances working out the way you want that you become depressed, angry, and feel sorry for yourself if they do not? Do you give your expectations to God by telling Him, "Lord, You are good and however You decide to work this out for Your glory, I thank You."

4. A thankful person is a joy to be around.

    Do others seek to be around you because you are a grateful, cheerful person or do they avoid you because they are tired of hearing you complain? Do you grumble and complain about the least little things — the weather, your hair, your husband, your children, your job, your church, your friends? ... How would others describe you — always complaining or always grateful to God?

5. A thankful person is able to worship God as He deserves and desires.

> Are you like the Psalmist who praised the LORD and gave thanks to the LORD with all his heart? (Psalm 111:1-4). When you are at church, do you sincerely give thanks to God as you sing His praises and hear His Word read and preached? Do you view God's creation as wonderful and marvelous and are you grateful for it? Do you view minor little annoyances in your life as little tests from God and do you thank Him for them? In your thoughts and prayers, do you bow before the Lord in awe and thanksgiving as you worship Him?

In my eight years of counseling women at the Atlanta Biblical Counseling Center, there were a handful of ladies that I would describe as "deeply disturbed." Even though their life circumstances were all different, they had one common characteristic, they were not grateful to God and they were not persuaded of His goodness. We must think right thoughts about God not only to be emotionally stable but also to give Him great glory and honor. As we submit ourselves to God's plan for our lives, we are to thank Him daily not just for the food we eat but for every small or large test or trial that comes our way. Won't you take some time now to stop reading and pray and thank God?

The Attitude of a Forbearing Heart

"You're making me nervous!" "Hurry up!" "I can't stand it!" "Why would anyone want to paint their living room white when they could paint it green?" "If those little children run across my yard one more time, I'm going to scream!" "I would never act like he does!" People who think and respond like this are intolerant of others. They are especially intolerant of those who have different opinions or ideas as well as those who have sinful weaknesses that they do not have. On the other hand, a person who is *forbearing is tolerant*. In other words, *they put up with differences and biblically bear with the sin and mistakes of others.*

Forbearance is not a word that we use much these days but according to the Bible, it is important. So, let's take the time to study the attitude of a forbearing heart.

Biblical Principles on The Attitude of a Forbearing Heart

1. God demonstrated His righteousness by showing His forbearance.

   But now apart from the Law the righteousness of God has been manifested, being witnessed by the Law and the Prophets, even the righteousness of God through faith in Jesus Christ for all those who believe; for there is no distinction; for all have sinned and fall short of the glory of God, being justified as a gift by His grace through the redemption which is in Christ Jesus; whom God displayed publicly as a propitiation in His blood through faith. <u>This was to demonstrate His righteousness, because in the forbearance of God He passed over the sins previously committed; for the demonstration, I say; of His righteousness at the present time, so that He might be just and the justifier of the one who has faith in Jesus.</u>
   Romans 3:21-26, emphasis added

2. We are to be tolerant of one another as we work hard at having unity.

   I therefore, the prisoner of the Lord, entreat you to walk in a manner worthy of the calling with which you have been called, with all humility and gentleness, with patience, <u>showing tolerance to one another in love,</u> being diligent to preserve the unity of the Spirit in the bond of peace.
   Ephesians 4:1-3, emphasis added

3. We are to bear with one another.

   So, as those who have been chosen of God, holy and beloved, put on a heart of compassion, kindness, humility, gentleness and patience; <u>bearing with one another,</u> and forgiving each other, whoever has a complaint against anyone; just as the Lord forgave you, so also should you.
   Colossians 3:12-13, emphasis added

---

4. Our forbearance should be known to all.

Let your forbearing spirit be known to all men. The Lord is near. **Philippians 4:5**

Practical Ways to have a Forbearing Heart

1. We are to follow the example of the Lord Jesus Christ that even though He was tempted, He never sinned. (See Hebrews 4:15.)

   When tempted to react to another's sin, instead of thinking, "I can't stand this!", do you think, "By God's grace I not only *can* stand this but I can try to help the other person." Do you put up with minor, petty little annoyances or do they really bother you? When suffering for righteousness sake, do you forbear throughout the circumstances?

2. We are likely to become intolerant when we begin to judge motives.

   Are you guilty of thinking judgmental thoughts far beyond what the situation allows or do you stick to the facts and give the benefit of the doubt? Do you forbear with the mistakes of others or do you become frustrated and angry?

3. We need to be accepting of differences that we have — likes and dislikes, ways to rear our children, our time schedule and husband's time schedule.

   Do you have strong, dogmatic opinions about matters that are really insignificant? When tempted to say something critical, do you stop and think, "It is alright if he has a different opinion since it is not a sin issue."

4. God puts difficult people in our lives always for a purpose. One of His purposes is to make us more godly.

   When confronted with an unbeliever who does not have the same standards you have, would you likely think, "I can't stand it any more!" or would you think, "She is not a Christian, she has no capacity to think as a Christian." Is your **"forbearing spirit known to all** [even difficult] **men?"** (Philippians 4:5, adaptation added).

5. We choose to glorify God by being forbearing or we choose to sin.

   When circumstances do not go your way, do you resort to angry bullying and threats in order to have your way? Do you have a calming effect in chaos or do you contribute to it because you do not bear up under it well? What is more important to you — expressing your frustration or glorifying God?

6. Forbearance and overlooking sin in the name of "letting love cover" are two different things.

   Do you forbear with others while at the same time you respond biblically in love with careful, measured responses to their sin? (See Galatians 6:1.) Or do you try to ignore sin in the name of "letting love cover" until you cannot stand it any longer?

Often the passage **"Above all keep fervent in your love for one another because love covers a multitude of sins"** (1Peter 4:8) is understood to mean that we are to forbear until we cannot stand it any longer. However, overlooking sin by ignoring it or saying nothing is not what the 1 Peter 4 passage means. Pastor Stuart Scott explains what "love covers a multitude of sins" means:

> As best I understand it, "love covers (or conceals) a multitude of sins" means, love does not take into consideration, bring up, or share sins that have already been dealt with. So the answer to the question, "Do we cover sin?" is a definite, "Yes." We deal with it, and then we must cover it. If we do not hide (from others and ourselves) our wife's [or other people's] sin after it has been dealt with, we have not truly forgiven her [them].
>
> Since overlooking or passing over a transgression cannot mean to live in some sort of non-reality as if nothing happened and it cannot mean to let our wife [others] believe that her [their] sin is not a problem, it must mean something else. To overlook means while you have indeed been personally offended, you chose not to react on the basis of that fact, but deal with the offense with patience and graciousness, because you are looking more to the glory of God and the good of the other person. Our need to initially "overlook" our own injury does not release us from our own duty to hold our wives [and other Christians] accountable for sin.[43] (Adaptation added)

Summary of the Attitude of a Forbearing Heart

A person who is forbearing puts up with the differences as well as mistakes of others and they biblically bear with the sin of others. Instead of thinking or yelling, "You're making me nervous!", their thoughts are "How can I help them?" Instead of "Hurry up!", it's "I would do this quicker but I can forbear with their slowness and wait." Instead of "Why would anyone want to paint their living room white when they could paint it green?" it's "It's their living room and it's OK if they paint it white." Instead of "If those little children run across my yard one more time, I'm going to scream!" it's "It's OK for me to not want the children running across the yard but putting up with their childishness is much more important than my sinning. I will speak to them but calmly and in love."

Those who are forbearing are like the Lord Jesus who had to put up with more than we can ever imagine. They work hard at having unity in the church and at home. They bear with one another and forgive. Their forbearance is obvious to others, including unbelievers. They do not judge motives and are accepting of the non-sinful differences that they have with others. They do not ignore sin but they handle it biblically and thus, they are like their Lord. Forbearance is an important biblical concept and by God's grace they will "put on" the heart's attitude of forbearance.

Chapter Conclusion

Do you remember reading about Daisy the Dog in the introduction to this chapter? Daisy was learning by rote automatic responses to be obedient, content, grateful, and forbearing. In addition, she was enabling others to be a servant. I visited Anna and Tony recently and am still not impressed with Daisy's progress. All is not in vain, however, because it seems that the Lord is working in Anna's and Tony's and the children's character through Daisy's disobedience.

Daisy will never receive an eternal reward from the Lord Jesus for her obedience, but Anna and Tony will in their relationships with others. As they obey by faith and because they love the Lord, His commands will not be a burden. As they are content in their circumstances and focus on seeking God and pleasing Him, they will not complain. And finally as they desire to be and show in their actions that they are voluntary servants to the Lord, they will not allow themselves to be emotionally enslaved to others and they will faithfully show their servant's heart by their deeds. The more that Anna and Tony become like Christ, the less they will be **"conformed to this world"** and the more they will have godly heart's attitudes that have been **"transformed by the renewing of [their] minds"** (Romans 12:2, adaptations added].

As we continue to learn about the attitudes of our heart, we will see in the next chapter the attitude of a pure heart.

Chapter 11

Study Questions

1.Match the following:

An obedient person puts God's desires ahead of their own desires.	1 John 5:3
Instead of being conformed to our former lusts, we are to be holy like God.	1 John 2:3-5
We are to obey God even if we must suffer for it.	1 Peter 1:14-16
Obedience is one of the evidences of salvation.	Matthew 26:39
For those who love the Lord, His commands are not a burden.	Acts 5:27-29

2. Reread the questions on pages 164-165 concerning "Practical Ways to have an Obedient Heart." Take your time and think about each question and give an honest answer. For those areas in which you know you need to improve, write out several practical ways that you should think and respond the next time.

3. Match the following:

We can learn to be content in our circumstances because God will help us.	1 Corinthians 10:9-10
It will help me to be content if I focus on seeking God and pleasing Him.	Job 1:20-22
True contentment means we do not have to sin against God.	Matthew 6:25,33
A person who is content does not grumble about their circumstances.	1 Timothy 6:8
Christians are to be content with the necessities of life.	Philippians 4:11-13

4. Reread the questions on pages 167-168 concerning "Practical Ways to have a Contented Heart." Take your time and think about each question and give an honest answer. For those areas in which you know you need to improve, write out several practical ways that you should think and respond the next time.

5. Match the following:

Those with a servant's heart will be rewarded by God.	1 Corinthians 7:23
We should be a servant to others because we are a servant of the Lord Jesus.	John 15:20
If you are truly the Lord Jesus' servant, there will be times you will suffer persecution.	2 Timothy 2:24-26
We are not to be slaves of men.	Matthew 20:25-28
The Lord's bond-servant is not to quarrel but to be kind instead.	Colossians 1:7-8

6. Reread the questions on pages 171-172 concerning "Practical Ways to have a Servant's Heart." Take your time and think about each question and give an honest answer. For those areas in which you know you need to improve, write out several practical ways that you should think and respond the next time.

7. Match the following:

We are to be exceedingly thankful for God's gift of grace to us, the Lord Jesus Christ.	Psalm 100:1-5
Expressing gratitude is part of worshiping God.	Colossians 3:15
Unbelievers are not grateful to God.	2 Corinthians 9:15
We are commanded in Scripture to be thankful.	Job 1:21
We are to be thankful for whatever God brings our way.	Romans 1:21

8. Reread the questions on pages 175-176 concerning "Practical Ways to have a Grateful Heart." Take your time and think about each question and give an honest answer. For those areas in which you know you need to improve, write out several practical ways that you should think and respond the next time.

9. Match the following:

God demonstrated His righteousnessby showing His forbearance.	Colossians 3:12-13
One of the characteristics we must have in order to have unity with others is forbearance.	Philippians 4:5
Christians are to "put on" bearing with one another.	Ephesians 4:1-3
Both believers and unbelievers who know us should see our forbearance.	Romans 3:21-26

10. Reread the questions on pages 178-179 concerning "Practical Ways to have a Forbearing Heart." Take your time and think about each question and give an honest answer. For those areas in which you know you need to improve, write out several practical ways that you should think and respond the next time.

Chapter 12

The Attitudes of a Pure Heart

Recently my pastor, John Crotts, and I had an opportunity to counsel a young couple involved in pornography and adultery. It was particularly devastating to hear the details and the ease with which they justified their sin. John, who is much younger than I am, asked me if during the 1960's sexual revolution it was as easy for people to fall in and out of bed with each other as it is today. I told him, "No. I remember graduating from high school in the sixties and can think of three girls out of hundreds who became pregnant out of wedlock (abortions were illegal). All three of them quietly quit school and married the father of their child. Many of my friends, even though they were probably not Christians, were virgins when they married. When you heard of someone's parents getting a divorce or one parent running off with another man or woman, it was rare and shocking. Sexually explicit acts that are routine news reports now were unspeakable and mostly unknown back then. The beginnings of the sexual revolution in America via the influence of the Playboy Philosophy in the 1960's was only the seed of what we see today."

America today is very much like Corinth was back in the Apostle Paul's day. In Corinth, sexual promiscuity was accepted as a way of life. Worshipers paid money to temple prostitutes to have sex in order to appease their gods. The people from Corinth who had become Christians are described by Paul in 1 Corinthians 5:9 as *former* fornicators, adulterers, effeminates, and homosexuals (1 Corinthians 6:9-11). Yet they had been washed clean from their sin and thus described as **"...such were some of you."** (1 Corinthians 6:11). Just as in the wicked city of Corinth, nothing is more challenged by the world today than the virtue of purity. But in spite of the challenge, our bodies are still to be used for God's glory and the older women are still to **"teach and encourage the younger women ...to be pure"** (Titus 2:5).

God's standard of sexual purity is clearly spelled out in Scripture. In the Old Testament, His standard is seen in the Ten Commandments. In the New Testament, His standard is seen in the Sermon on the Mount. This chapter will explain God's moral standard in the Old and New Testaments, list ten biblical principles concerning sex, and consider several specific sexual sins and their antidote. We will begin with God's moral standard in the Old and New Testament.

God's Moral Standard in the Old and New Testaments

"You shall not commit adultery" (Exodus 20:14). **"You shall not covet your neighbor's wife..."** (Exodus 20:17). God's high and holy standard regarding sex was clearly and plainly given to the nation of Israel by God Himself through Moses. They were God's special, covenant people and He wanted them to be holy and remain holy. So holy in fact that they were to purge the nation permanently of those who did not hold to God's sexual standard.

> *If a man is found lying with a married woman, then both of them shall die, the man who lay with the woman, and the woman; thus you shall purge the evil from Israel. If there is a girl who is a virgin engaged to a man, and another man finds her in the city and lies with her, then you shall bring them both out to the gate of that city and you shall stone them to death; the girl, because she did not cry out in the city, and the man, because he has violated his neighbor's wife. Thus you shall purge the evil from among you.* **Deuteronomy 22:23-24**

By the time the Lord Jesus came to earth, the Pharisees had devised many ways to get around God's standard. They still held to the technicality of the law **"You shall not commit adultery"** (Exodus 20:14) but somehow **"You shall not covet your neighbor's wife"** was lost in the shuffle. The Lord Jesus was referring to the Pharisees' convenient interpretation of God's law when He said in the Sermon on the Mount, **"You have heard that it was said, 'YOU SHALL NOT COMMIT ADULTERY'"** but I say to you that everyone who looks at a woman with lust for her has already committed adultery with her in his heart"** (Matthew 5:27-28).

It was not only the physical act of sexual intercourse but also the mental attitude of the heart's desire that Jesus condemns in Matthew chapter five.

Mental impurity is the seed of physical impurity. Many times mentally adulterous couples or fornicating couples pride themselves on not having technically had sex, yet in their hearts they imagine it, desire it, or go as far as they can without that one little, final technicality. As far as God is concerned, they are guilty and must repent.

If a Christian will not repent of sexual sin, they are to be disciplined out of the church. Jesus explained the process in Matthew 18.

> *If your brother sins, go and reprove him in private; and if he listens to you, you have won your brother. But if he does not listen to you, take one or two more with you, so that BY THE MOUTH OF TWO OR THREE WITNESSES EVERY FACT MAY BE CONFIRMED. If he refuses to listen to them, tell it to the church; and if he refuses to listen even to the church, let him be to you as a Gentile and a tax-gatherer. Truly I say to you, whatever you bind on earth shall have been bound in heaven; and whatever you loose on earth shall have been loosed in heaven.*
> *Matthew 18:15-18*

Being disciplined out of the church until the immoral person repents is God's way of keeping His church pure and purging the evil from the church. Paul gives a specific example of a man in the church in Corinth who was committing incest with his father's wife. Not only that, the people in the church knew it and were tolerating it. Paul was very clear when he wrote, **"not to associate with any so-called brother if he is an immoral person...not even to eat with such a one. For what have I to do with judging outsiders? Do you not judge those who are within the church? But those who are outside, God judges. REMOVE THE WICKED MAN FROM AMONG YOURSELVES"** (1 Corinthians 5:11-12). Sexual immorality is wrong and Christians are to make judgments on such issues. If the person will not turn from their sin, they are to be disciplined by the church. If they really are a Christian, God will not leave them alone in their sin. Paul told the church at Corinth, **"I have decided to deliver such a one to Satan for the destruction of his flesh, so that his spirit may be saved in the day of the Lord Jesus"** (1 Corinthians 5:5). The extreme consequences of sexual sin were not only for the time of the Old Testament but also are consistent with the character of God for the New Testament time.

Because of our natural, deceitful hearts and our Corinthian culture, it is all the more imperative that we know and take seriously what the Scriptures have to teach us about sexual sin.

Ten Biblical Principles Concerning Sexual Sin

1. It is God's will that we be pure.

    > *For this is the will of God, your sanctification; that is, that you abstain from sexual immorality... For God has not called us for the purpose of impurity, but in sanctification.* **1 Thessalonians 4:3,7**

    Apparently the behavior of some of the members of the church in Thessalonica was causing Paul some concerns, so he wrote them to address several issues. One of these issues was sexual immorality, and typically, Paul was very straightforward. He did not vaguely tiptoe around the issue. He requested and exhorted them to walk in a way that would please God. He reminded them, **"For you know what commandments we gave you by the authority of the Lord Jesus"** (1 Thessalonians 4:2). And he wrote, **"For this is the will of God..."**

    Since God created Adam and Eve, it has been and always will be *God's will* that we be sexually pure. Each and every generation must be reminded of this fact. I heard of one pastor who was committing adultery who said, "If I can just have one week of happiness with my lover, it will have been worth it." How incredibly pathetic! He lost his family. She lost her family. He lost his job. And in a very short time, he lost his lover. He loved his sin more than he loved the Lord or his family.

    When God calls us out of darkness into His marvelous light, He expects us to walk in that light. He expects us to be set apart or sanctified in the truth. He expects us to abstain from sexual immorality. There is no doubt that it is God's will that we be pure.

2. We are to be in control of our bodies.

    > *...that each of you know how to possess his own vessel in sanctification and honor, not in lustful passion, like the Gentiles who do not know God...*
    > **1 Thessalonians 4:4,5**

    Your "vessel" is referring to your physical body. You are to be, at all times, in control of what your body is doing. What we do with our bodies – the signals we give off by the clothes we wear (or don't wear), the way our eyes catch the eyes of a man — are signs of sensuality and are deeds of the flesh. And if sensuality is a sin then how much more sinful is fornication and adultery! Christians are not to be like the world. Their values and desires are different. We should control our bodies in a God-honoring way, not in lustful passion as those who do not know God.

3. Immoral people will be punished.

> *...and that no man transgress and defraud his brother in the matter because <u>the Lord is the avenger in all these things</u>, just as we also told you before and solemnly warned you.*   *1 Thessalonians 4:6, emphasis added*

The Scriptures talk about evil, darkness, things hidden in the darkness, and the deeds of darkness. Sexual sin fits perfectly into those categories and often it is done under the cover of darkness in secret places where no one can see. But God sees and He may stay His hand of judgment for a time, but ultimately it will come. The things hidden will be brought to light and perfect justice will come from God's hand. The unbeliever who is an adulterer, fornicator, or homosexual, someday will know personally what it is to die, and as Hebrews tells us, **"after this comes judgment"** (Hebrews 9:27). Immoral people will be punished.

4. It is not good for a man to sexually arouse a woman except, of course, for a husband and wife.

> *Now concerning the things about which you wrote, it is good for a man not to touch a woman.*
> *1 Corinthians 7:1*

Paul is in the middle of a section in his letter to the church at Corinth on sexual immorality. He has been telling them to give God glory in this area of their lives. In Chapter seven, he specifically teaches them about sexual relations in marriage. When he wrote, **"... it is good for a man not to touch a woman,"** he seems to be referring to a man and woman who are not married to each other. He should not touch her in any way that would arouse her sexually. Neither should she touch him in that way.

Sometimes women are naive or act as if they are naive about what arouses a man. I know of one Christian woman who was known to give the men in the church lingering, tight hugs. In fact, several of the men complained. When she was told by one of the elders that her hugs were a problem, she stopped — much to everyone's relief!

It is common for single adults or teenagers to ask the question, "How far is too far?" A good answer would be, "We should not think in terms of 'How far?'"

Instead, we should think, 'How would God have me think about sex? Anything that causes sexual arousal outside of marriage is too far.'" It does not take much for a man or a woman to become sexually aroused, so it is better not to start anything. Every Christian should decide firmly in their own mind ahead of time that they will not allow themselves to be tempted at all in that way. It is like poking a small little hole in the dam to let just a little bit of water out and then being surprised when the entire dam comes tumbling down. Except for husband and wife, they are not to sexually arouse others.

5.   Your sexual desires are to be met by your spouse.

> *But because of immoralities, each man is to have his own*
> *wife, and each woman is to have her own husband.*
> *1 Corinthians 7:2*

Sexual desires do not have to be sinful. In fact, God pronounced all that He had created **"very good"** (Genesis 1:31). It is only when those desires are outside the realm of marriage that they become sinful. Husbands and wives are to go to each other when they experience such desires. For those whose spouse is out of town or perhaps sick in the hospital, they must by God's grace exercise self-control. Marriage is one of God's means to help prevent temptation to sin sexually. For those in the immoral city of Corinth, Paul reminds them that sexual desires are to be met for a man by his wife and a wife by her husband.

6.   Lustful sexual thoughts are sinful.

> *But the things that proceed out of the mouth come from*
> *the heart, and those defile the man. For out of the heart*
> *come <u>evil thoughts</u>, murders, <u>adulteries</u>, <u>fornications</u>,*
> *thefts, false witness, slanders. These are things which*
> *defile the man; but to eat with unwashed hands does not*
> *defile the man.   Matthew 15:18-20, emphasis added*

Religious people think that their rules and traditions are what make and keep them holy. For instance, the Pharisees had an elaborate hand-washing routine before they ate. Because the disciples did not adhere to their hand-washing ritual, the Pharisees accused them of being unclean. The Lord Jesus corrected their heresy by explaining that it is man's heart (thoughts, choices, desires) that defile him, not the manner in which they wash their hands. Adulteries and fornications begin with our sinful dispositions which then influence our thoughts, then those thoughts are acted upon. It is not only outward acts of immorality that are sinful but also lustful sexual thoughts.

7. God forgives any sexual sin at the moment of salvation.

> *Or do you not know that the unrighteous shall not in-*
> *herit the kingdom of God? Do not be deceived; neither*
> *fornicators, nor idolaters, nor adulterers, nor effeminate,*
> *nor homosexuals, nor thieves, nor the covetous, nor*
> *drunkards, nor revilers, nor swindlers, will inherit the*
> *kingdom of God. <u>Such were some of you;</u> but you were*
> *<u>washed,</u> but you were <u>sanctified,</u> but you were <u>justified</u>*
> *in the name of the Lord Jesus Christ and in the Spirit of*
> *our God.   1 Corinthians 6:9-11, emphasis added*

No longer did the words fornicators, adulterers, effeminate, or homosexuals describe the believers in the Corinthian church. Instead, they had been washed clean of their sin by the blood of the Lamb, and had begun the process of being made holy by God. They were no longer enemies of God, but legally declared right before Him. They were wrapped in the robes of Christ's righteousness because He bore their sins in His body on the cross. Like all the other sin they had committed and would commit until they died, their sins were forgiven and God the Father's wrath was appeased.

8. We are to run from immorality.

> *Do you not know that your bodies are members of Christ?*
> *Shall I then take away the members of Christ and make*
> *them members of a harlot? May it never be! Or do you*
> *not know that the one who joins himself to a harlot is*
> *one body with her? For He says, "THE TWO SHALL BE-*
> *COME ONE FLESH." But the one who joins himself to*
> *the Lord is one spirit with Him. Flee immorality. Every*
> *other sin that a man commits is outside the body, but the*
> *immoral man sins against his own body. Or do you not*
> *know that your body is a temple of the Holy Spirit who*
> *is in you, whom you have from God, and that you are*
> *not your own? For you have been bought with a price:*
> *therefore glorify God in your body.*
> *   1 Corinthians 6:15-20*

What might be a temptation for one person may not be a temptation for another, but sexual immorality is not one temptation that you want to put to the test. Think about Joseph and the story of Potiphar's wife. Joseph was Potiphar's slave and had been entrusted to manage Potiphar's household. Potiphar's wife had other plans for Joseph as she tried to seduce him. Joseph did the only wise and honorable thing he could do — he rapidly fled the scene (Genesis 39:6-13). He did not hang around to see how long he could withstand the temptation. Apparently he did not rehearse a sexual scene in his mind imagining what it would be like to be with her. Instead, he thought about how it would be a grievous sin against God and against Potiphar. He ran just as we are to run from immorality (2 Timothy 2:22; 1 Corinthians 6:18).

9. Homosexuality is a form of perverted sexual lust.

> *Therefore, God gave them over in the lusts of their hearts to impurity, so that their bodies would be dishonored among them. For they exchanged the truth of God for a lie, and worshiped and served the creature rather than the Creator, who is blessed forever. Amen. For this reason God gave them over to degrading passions; for their women exchanged the natural function for that which is unnatural, and in the same way also the men abandoned the natural function of the woman and burned in their desire toward one another, men with men committing indecent acts and receiving in their own persons the due penalty of their error. And just as they did not see fit to acknowledge God any longer, God gave them over to a depraved mind, to do those things which are not proper...*
> *Romans 1:24-28*

Think for a minute about the descriptions of the homosexual in Romans chapter one. They are characterized by degrading passions, believing lies, worshiping and serving the creature, burning with unnatural passion, committing indecent acts, and doing things that are not proper. They also have been given over to a depraved mind by God. The whole list is disturbing, but especially the part about being given over by God. Their spiritual blindness is huge and very dark. I have counseled homosexual women who after hearing me read Romans chapter one were unmoved and said casually, "I know all that. That doesn't convince me. Can't you think of some other passages?" It really would not have mattered if I had read every verse in the entire Bible that spoke of homosexuality — unless God lifted the veil of sin from their eyes, they would not be able to see.

A depraved mind is one that thinks evil, corrupt, perverted thoughts. It is a result of rejecting God and worshiping and serving the creature rather than the Creator. It results in inordinate passions and extreme jealousy. It will cause women to leave their husbands and children and burn in desire for other women. There is no "polite" way to describe it. Homosexuality is a form of perverted sexual lust.

10. Seven reasons why adultery is especially serious.

(1) Adultery violates the "one flesh" principle.

For this cause a man shall leave his father and his mother, and cleave to his wife; and they shall become one flesh.
Genesis 2:24

Or do you not know that the one who joins himself to a harlot is one body with her? For He says, "THE TWO SHALL BECOME ONE FLESH."   *1 Corinthians 6:16*

(2) Adultery can utterly destroy a person.

The one who commits adultery with a woman is lacking sense; he who would destroy himself does it.
Proverbs 6:32

(3) Adultery can cause spiritual and physical death.

To deliver you from the strange woman, from the adulteress who flatters with her words; that leaves the companion of her youth and forgets the covenant of her God. For her house sinks down to death and her tracks lead to the dead; none who go to her return again, nor do they reach the paths of life.   *Proverbs 2:16-19*

(4) Adultery can be destructive to a physical relationship with your spouse.

Drink water from your own cistern and fresh water from your own well. Should your springs be dispersed abroad, streams of water in the streets? Let them be yours alone and not for strangers with you. Let your fountain be blessed, and rejoice in the wife of your youth. As a loving hind and a graceful doe, let her breasts satisfy you at all times; be exhilarated always with her love.
Proverbs 5:15-19

(5) Adultery obscures the nature of righteous love.

Love ... does not act unbecomingly; it does not seek its own, ... does not rejoice in unrighteousness, but rejoices with the truth.   *1 Corinthians 13:5-6*

(6) Adultery violates the fact that marriage pictures Christ and the church.

Husbands, love your wives, just as Christ also loved the church and gave Himself up for her, so that He might sanctify her, having cleansed her by the washing of water with the word, that He might present to Himself the church in all her glory, having no spot or wrinkle or any such thing; but that she would be holy and blameless.
Ephesians 5:25-27

(7) Adultery spawns other sins such as jealousy, lies, murder, and strife.

For jealousy enrages a man, and he will not spare in the day of vengeance.   *Proverbs 6:34*

There are six things which the LORD hates, yes, seven which are an abomination to Him: haughty eyes, a lying tongue, and hands that shed innocent blood, a heart that devises wicked plans, feet that run rapidly to evil, a false witness who utters lies, and one who spread strife among brothers.   *Proverbs 6:16-19*

Now that we have seen several biblical principles concerning sexual relations, let's turn our attention to some specific sins and their biblical antidote.

Specific Sexual Sins

1. Lust is a mental attitude sin of desiring and/or envisioning the sex act with someone other than your spouse.

2. Sensuality is acting in a way that entices another to desire you sexually. Women often do this by how they look into men's eyes, catching them with a longing, sensual gaze (See Proverbs 6:24-25).

3. Masturbation is self-gratification to the point of sexual release. Self-gratification is unloving since the focus is on self instead of love for your spouse. It is accompanied by lustful thoughts.

4. Fornication is the sex act between an unmarried man and an unmarried woman.

5. Adultery is sexual intercourse with someone other than your spouse.

6. Perversions include homosexuality and incest. Homosexuality is unnatural affections and sex acts between members of the same sex. Incest is sexual relations between family members who are not husband and wife.

The Biblical Antidote to Sexual Sin

Put off sexual sin by putting on the Lord Jesus Christ. In other words, think and act as our Lord would. He would never plan to entice someone sexually by what He was wearing or the perfume He put on. His thoughts would only be pure and wholesome towards the other person. He would only want to draw them to greater and greater godliness.	**Let us behave properly as in the day, not in carousing and drunkenness, not in sexual promiscuity and sensuality, not in strife and jealousy. But put on the Lord Jesus Christ, and make no provision for the flesh in regard to its lusts.** **Romans 13:13-14**
Make no provision for the flesh. Provisions for the flesh are things that would tempt or entice you to sin. Some of the common provisions for women are romantic novels, the internet, soap operas, certain movies and songs, being around a particular man that you find yourself thinking of too often or in a way that you know you should not, and pornography. Obviously, any of these provisions for the flesh would make it difficult to keep your thoughts pure and you would be much more likely to engage in sensuality or sexual sin.	**But put on the Lord Jesus Christ, and make no provision for the flesh in regard to its lusts.** **Romans 13:14**

Analyze your thoughts to see if they are pure. A pure thought does not lead to lust. It is a thought that would stand the scrutiny of God and pass the test. Pure thoughts give God great glory and you would not be embarrassed to have them shown on the video screen for all the world to see. Be honest as you analyze your thoughts. Only the Lord and you know if they truly are pure.	**Finally, brethren, what is true, whatever is honorable, whatever is right, whatever is pure, whatever is lovely, whatever is of good repute, if there is any excellence and if anything worthy of praise, let your mind dwell on these things.** **Philippians 4:8**
Clear your conscience. Often women think they can handle their sexual sin all by themselves. What often happens is that years later they are still thinking, "Hey, I can handle this." Our pride hinders us from seeking accountability. Instead, clear your conscience by asking forgiveness of those you have directly sinned against and seek accountability from a godly, older woman or your husband to think, dress, and act in a God-honoring way. Once you have cleared your conscience, it will be much more difficult for you to continue to sin in that way. (One word of caution, be wise in how much you share with those holding you accountable. They need to know basic facts but they do not need to know sordid, graphic details lest they would be tempted to think wrongly.)	**If we confess our sins, He is faithful and righteous to forgive us our sins and to cleanse us from all unrighteousness. 1 John 1:9** **If therefore you are presenting your offering at the altar, and there remember that your brother has something against you, leave your offering there before the altar and go your way; first be reconciled to your brother, and then come and present your offering.** **Matthew 5:23-24**

Memorize Scripture and tell yourself the Scripture instead of the lustful scenarios in your mind. If you do not know which Scriptures to memorize, choose several from this chapter. Plan ahead what you are going to tell yourself the next time you are tempted to think wrongly. Until you have the Scripture memorized, write it on index cards and carry it with you so that you can read it until you have committed it to memory. You also can pray for others. Prayer is a very good use of your mind and is very honoring to the Lord.

Thy word I have treasured in my heart, that I may not sin against You.   Psalm 119:11

Finally then, brethren, we request and exhort you in the Lord Jesus, that as you received from us instruction as to how you ought to walk and please God (just as you actually do walk), that you excel still more. For you know what commandments we gave you by the authority of the Lord Jesus. For this is the will of God, your sanctification; that is, that you abstain from sexual immorality; that each of you know how to possess his own vessel in sanctification and honor, not in lustful passion, like the Gentiles who do not know God and that no man transgress and defraud his brother in the matter because the Lord is the avenger in all these things, just as we also told you before and solemnly warned you. For God has not called us for the purpose of impurity, but in sanctification. Consequently, he who rejects this is not rejecting man but the God who gives His Holy Spirit to you.
                    1 Thessalonians 4:1-8

Flee immorality and guard your heart. Women need to be careful with the friendships they make. Men friends, other than your husband, should be superficial friends from an emotional standpoint and as a brother-sister relationship from a physical standpoint. Work at building friendships with women and not men. Do not complain about your husband to one of the men at church or work. If your husband is sinning, there are righteous, biblical ways to handle it. If you find yourself thinking about a particular man too much or thinking about how you want to dress or fix your hair when you know he will be around, repent right away and do not continue to make provisions for the flesh. Also do not allow a man/friend to pour his heart out to you concerning how difficult his wife is. Only a fool would listen to just his side of that story! Flee immorality while it is still at the early "I'm thinking about this" stage. Guard your heart and keep it pure for Jesus' sake.

Flee immorality. Every other sin that a man commits is outside the body, but the immoral man sins against his own body. Or do you not know that your body is a temple of the Holy Spirit who is in you, whom you have from God, and that you are not your own? For you have been bought with a price: therefore glorify God in your body.

1 Corinthians 6:18-20

Meditate on the cross and on the outcome of sin. Take the time to think about the sin for which you have been forgiven. It is a very sobering thought, isn't it? Now think about sin and the devastating effects it can have on your loved ones. Lastly, think about the Lord Jesus and His agony on the

Let no one say when he is tempted, "I am being tempted by God"; for God cannot be tempted by evil, and He Himself does not tempt anyone. But each one is tempted when he is carried away and enticed by his own lust. Then when lust has conceived, it gives birth to sin; and when sin is

cross as He bore your sins. Certainly it does not take long to realize the momentary pleasures of sexual lust are not worth the price that had to be paid. Do you love the Lord? Do you desire Him above all others? Do you want to be a godly person who is chaste and pure? It will help you greatly if you meditate on the cross and on the outcome of sin.	**accomplished, it brings forth death. Do not be deceived, my beloved brethren.** **James 1:13-16** **He was pierced through for our transgressions, He was crushed for our iniquities; the chastening for our well-being fell upon Him, and by His scourging we are healed. All of us like sheep have gone astray, each of us has turned to his own way; but the LORD has caused the iniquity of us all to fall on Him.** **Isaiah 53:5-6**

Conclusion

We do live in a Corinthian culture. The sexual revolution of the sixties was almost insignificant compared to what is happening today. Please take this seriously and if you are sensual, immodest, adulterous, or in any way immoral, get down on your knees and earnestly pray for forgiveness, seek accountability, work diligently on thinking pure thoughts, and memorizing Scripture. For those Christians in Corinth who previously were immoral they were made new and clean by the blood of the Lamb of God. Scripture does not tell us but it would not surprise me if they had the attitude that I now have - I would rather the Lord Jesus take me home to be with Him than for me to dishonor Him in that way ever again. No matter what your background or what you have done, with God's help, you can be **"transformed by the renewing of your mind"** into a pure and chaste child of God. What is your prayer?

∝∾

Chapter 12

Study Questions

1. According to Exodus 20:14 and Exodus 20:17, what is God's standard concerning sexual immorality?

2. What was supposed to happen to those who violated God's standard? See Deuteronomy 22:23-24.

3. How did the Pharisees hold to the technicality of God's Law but get around it in their hearts?

4. What is to happen today to the Christian who will not repent of sexual sin? See Matthew 18:15-18.

5. On what biblical basis are we to make judgments concerning sexual immorality? Give a Scripture reference to back up your answer.

6. From reading 1 Thessalonians 4:3,7, what is clearly God's will?

7. What kinds of "sensual signals" might people give off?

8. How might the Lord avenge immorality?
   See 1 Thessalonians 4:6 and Hebrews 9:27.

9. How would you answer the question concerning sexual relations between two people who are not married to each other, "How far is too far?" What Scripture would you show them?

10. How are sexual desires to be met? What if you are not married or your spouse cannot meet those desires?

11. According to what the Lord Jesus told the Pharisees, where does adultery and fornication originate?

12. How does God help those who used to be involved in sexual sin but have now become Christians? See 1 Corinthians 6:9-11.

13. Why is sexual sin particularly devastating?
    See 1 Corinthians 6:15-20.

14. What should you do if tempted?

15. How is the homosexual characterized according to Romans 1:24-28?

16. List several reasons why adultery is especially serious.

17. Why is masturbation sinful?

18. What does it mean to **"put on the Lord Jesus Christ and make no provision for the flesh"**? See Romans 13:13-14. List some practical steps to take. (For example: evaluate television and movies you watch and eliminate those that feed the flesh.)

19. Write down some examples of sexually impure thoughts you think (if, in fact, you do think impure thoughts. If not, skip this question) and beside each one write out a pure thought that would honor God.

20. Choose at least two Scriptures concerning sexual immorality to meditate on and to memorize. Work hard at this so that they will come readily to your mind.

21. If sexual temptation is a problem for you, it is so important that you do not justify what you are thinking and/or doing with thoughts like, "I won't do this again" or "I don't need someone to hold me accountable because I can handle it." Instead, pray about and then find an accountability partner who will help you. Many Christians forsake their outward sexual sin when they are saved but secretly hang onto their impure thoughts and desires. Please do not dishonor the Lord Jesus in this way.

22. If sexual lust is a problem for you, write out a detailed plan of Scripture memory, "put on" thoughts, and how you will talk to yourself the next time you are tempted. The Pharisees could not fool God and neither can you.
    What is your prayer?

Chapter 13

The Attitudes of A Loving Heart

When I was a child, my parents always saved the best Christmas present for last. Sometimes it would be hidden somewhere and I would temporarily be made to think that I had opened all my presents. Then someone would slyly say while reaching under the couch, "Oh, what's this?" And lo and behold, the best present ever was before me! In a similar way, I have saved the best heart's attitude for last. The attitude of a loving heart is the best because it is the most important. We know it is the most important because the Bible tells us it is the most important. If we do not have love, we are nothing. The greatest commandments in all of God's law are to love God and to love others. Just as my parents wanted to give me the very best present they could, *a person with a loving heart has a desire or acts towards another in a way that results in wanting the very best for that person.*

A loving heart is critical to pleasing God, so let's begin this section with nine biblical principles on the Attitude of a Loving Heart.

Biblical Principles on the Attitudes of a Loving Heart

1. We are to love God wholly and our neighbors as ourselves.

    > *One of them, a lawyer, asked Him a question, testing Him, "Teacher, which is the great commandment in the Law?" And He said to him, "You shall love the Lord your God with all your heart, and with all your soul, and with all your mind. This is the great and foremost commandment. The second is like it, You shall love your neighbor as yourself."* Matthew 22:35-40

The religious crowd in Jesus' day hated Him because His teachings exposed their pride and self-righteousness. So, they tried repeatedly to trick Him by asking Him questions. One of those questions was, "What is the great commandment in the Law?" That may seem to be an unusual question to us but for them it was logical. You see, they divided and subdivided all of God's Law into commands that were greater (and thus had to be kept) and those that were lesser (and thus were optional). Of course, God intended for them and for us to keep all of His commands, not just those the Pharisees considered most important. Jesus saw straight through their evil motives and got right at the heart of the matter when He summed up the greatest commandment — love God with every part of your being. In other words, our thoughts are to be on Him, our worship of Him alone, our greatest desire is to please Him and to serve Him. Love for God is to overshadow everything we think, say, or do as we honor Him through obedience to His Word – all of His Word, not just some of it.

The Lord then added a second greatest command to the first, **"Love your neighbor as you love yourself."** As we said, the Lord Jesus did not mean you have to first love yourself. It was understood that if we loved others as much as we love ourselves, it would be incredible how much we loved others. So, the first and foremost principle on having a heart's attitude of love is summed up magnificently by the Lord — love God with every part of your being and love others as you love yourself.

2. Love is a fruit of the Holy Spirit.

> *But the fruit of the Spirit is love...*   *Galatians 5:22*

I can vividly remember the first time as a new Christian that I responded in love to a particularly aggravating situation in contrast to my usual tendency to respond in anger. By the time this aggravating circumstance happened, I had learned about the fruit of the Spirit. Since my response was so contrary to the natural me, I knew it had to be a work of God and I was so excited that God was working in my heart. It is a supernatural grace gift from God to us when we show God's fruit in our life. Since none of us naturally put God and others first, it is easy to see how the Holy Spirit works in our life to enable us to show love to others.

3. Obedience proves love.

> *For this is the love of God, that we keep His commandments; and His commandments are not burdensome.*
> *1 John 5:3*

There is a sonnet that starts off "How do I love Thee? Let me count the ways..." Well, if you think about how many ways you are to love God, it is simple, there is only one way — by obeying Him. You can tell others all day long how much you love the Lord but unless you are obeying His commandments and your obedience is a joy for you and not a burden, then you do not really love Him. Not, that is, in a way that counts.

4. Our ability to love biblically comes from God and is an evidence of salvation.

> *Beloved, let us love one another, for love is from God;*
> *and everyone who loves is born of God and knows God.*
> *The one who does not love does not know God, for God*
> *is love...We love, because He first loved us.*
> *1 John 4:7,8,19*

The Lord Jesus told His disciples, **"A new commandment I give you, that you love one another,** *even as I have loved you,* **that you also love one another. By this all men will know that you are My disciples, if you have love for one another"** (John 13:34-35, emphasis added). The standard is – **"even as I have loved you."** Jesus' love is holy and sacrificial, not tainted with even a hint of selfishness. Obviously, neither the disciples nor believers today can love others as the Lord Jesus loved them *unless* God works in their heart and enables them. Christians know God and love others only because God loved them first.

5. Jesus' death on the cross is the supreme example of how love acts.

> *By this the love of God was manifested in us, that God*
> *has sent His only begotten Son into the world so that we*
> *might live through Him. In this is love, not that we loved*
> *God, but that He loved us and sent His Son to be the pro-*
> *pitiation for our sins.* *1 John 4:9-10*

There are probably few siblings who did not at least once while growing up endure a spanking that should have been given their brother or sister. Parents, who are less than perfect in their ability to discern what really happened, do sometimes realize later on that their punishment was unfair. It is probably nigh impossible for an "innocent" child to go through the punishment without loud, insistent, prior protest. Unlike the child, the Lord Jesus was a willing sacrifice. **"He was oppressed and He was afflicted, yet He did not open His mouth; like a lamb that is led to slaughter, and like a sheep that is silent** before its shearers, so He did not open His mouth" (Isaiah 53:7). When God the Father punished His beloved Son on the cross it was the only example ever of a completely sinless man suffering as He took the punishment that others deserved. **"As a result of the anguish of His soul, He [the Father] will see it and be satisfied..."** (Isaiah 53:11). The Father's wrath was satisfied or in other words, sin was propitiated. Jesus' death on the cross is the supreme example of how love acts.

6. Love is a mark of being a Christian and therefore we can have confidence in the day of judgment.

> *By this, love is perfected with us, so that we may have confidence in the day of judgment; because as He is, so also are we in this world. There is no fear in love; but perfect love casts out fear, because fear involves punishment, and the one who fears is not perfected in love.*
> **1 John 4:17-18**

"Judgment Day" is an expression that should put terror in the unbeliever's heart. The Bible tells about several judgments but the most famous one is the "great white throne judgment" (Revelation 20:11-15). At the great white throne judgment, God will judge unbelievers for their sin and **"if anyone's name was not found written in the book of life, he was thrown into the lake of fire"** (Revelation 20:15). Those who reject Christ should be terrified at the prospect. Christians, on the other hand, can look to that day with confidence. The reason, John says, that we can have confidence and not fear God's punishment is that God's **"love is perfected [completed] with us"** (1 John 4:17, explanation added). Our love for others is an evidence of our salvation and instead of fearing judgment and punishment, we can have confidence (1 John 4:18).

7. Our love for God is seen in our love for others.

> *If someone says, "I love God, " and hates his brother, he is a liar; for the one who does not love his brother whom he has seen, cannot love God whom he has not seen. And this commandment we have from Him, that the one who loves God should love his brother also.* **1 John 4:20-21**

Over and over in the letter of 1 John, the Apostle John writes about love: God's love for us and, in turn, our love for others. There is fruit in the life of a Christian that is produced in them by God. Their fruit goes far beyond mere lip service to loving others. John makes a vivid and direct connection between loving God and loving your brother. His words are a stern warning – **"If some-one says, 'I love God,' and hates his brother, he is a liar..."** (I John 4:20). Our love for God is seen in our love for others.

8. We are to love and pray for those who are against us.

> *You have heard that it was said, "You shall love your neighbor and hate your enemy." But I say to you, "love your enemies and pray for those who persecute you, in order that you may be sons of your Father who is in heaven; for He causes His sun to rise on the evil and the good, and sends rain on the righteous and the unrighteous. For if you love those who love you, what reward have you? Do not even the tax-gatherers do the same and if you greet your brothers only, what more are you doing than others? Do not even the Gentiles do the same? Therefore you are to be perfect, as your heavenly Father is perfect."*
>
> *Matthew 5:43-48*

In the Sermon on the Mount, the Lord Jesus refuted some of the Pharisees' teaching. Over and over, He said, **"You have heard that it was said"** (the Pharisees' twisted version of the Old Testament Scriptures), **"but I say to you..."** (Matthew 5:43-44). The Jewish hearers of His sermon had been taught by the Pharisees a wrong view of how to think about your enemies. The Pharisees had wrongly assumed that if you are to "love your neighbor" (their fellow Jews) then the opposite holds true – "hate your enemies." The Lord Jesus refuted the Pharisees by telling the people that instead of hating their enemies, they were to love them and pray for them.

God is kind and gracious not only to those who love Him but also to His enemies. The Christian is to be like God.

> The mark of perfection in the Christian is just this: his love is not determined by the loveliness or the attractiveness he finds in its object. His love is not conditional upon his being loved first. His love is not directed only towards those whose love he can rely on in return. No, his love is controlled by the knowledge that when he was God's enemy and a sinner, the Father first loved him. He is to show the Father's love, then he will "go and do likewise" (Luke 10:37).[44]

9.   We are to pursue love.

> ***Pursue love**, yet desire earnestly spiritual gifts, but especially that you may prophesy.*
> *1 Corinthians 14:1, emphasis added*

We pursue many different things over the course of our lives. Some we pursue with a great passion. It is not uncommon for someone to stay in school for years beyond high school in pursuit of a career. But how common is it for us to work that hard at pursuing love? As Christians we all want to be more loving but somehow it is just supposed to happen. Certainly God does His part by saving us and giving us an ability to love Him and others, but the question remains, are we doing our part? The Scriptures command us to love others.

But how, we ask, can we love in such a righteous and selfless way? First, we must keep in mind that our gracious heavenly Father provides His children every resource they need to obey His commands and to follow His example. We are divinely enabled to pay our great debt of love "because the love of God has been poured out within our hearts through the Holy Spirit who was given to us" (Romans 5:5). God's own love is the inexhaustible well from which, as it were, we can draw the supernatural love He commands us to live by. ...[45]

It is God who enables us to follow His command to "pursue love" and we should be diligently **"disciplining ourselves for the purpose of godliness"** (1 Timothy 4:7). In the next section, we will consider some practical examples of how to pursue love.

Application of the Attitudes of a Loving Heart

1.   If you love God, you put Him first.

If you love someone, you think about them often. You will desire to talk with them and plan ways to please them. What *you* want pales in comparison to what they would like. Likewise, if you love the Lord, you will think about Him often. You will talk with Him through prayer and plan ways to please Him. He will be the most important person in your life and you will strive to please Him, use your spiritual gifts, and give Him glory. You will be a daily living sacrifice for the Lord. If you love Him, you will put Him first.

2.   If you love others, you will be patient with them, kind to them, and demonstrate other responses spelled out in Scripture.

Some people seem to be more naturally loving than others. Whether you are one of these people or not, you are told repeatedly in Scriptures to **"pursue love"** and **"walk in love."** You do that by being patient, kind, etc. Take a few moments and ponder each of the following practical suggestions from 1 Corinthians 13 about "putting on" love.

Putting on Love [46]

1. "Love is patient."

It is common to become aggravated when things do not go our way, when something interferes with our plans, or when we do not feel well. However, by an act of our wills, we can be patient whether we feel like it or not. It is an active, humble, dependent choice to obey God in this manner. If we do, the Holy Spirit will help us by pouring out a measure of God's grace. One good way to develop the character quality of patience is to memorize Scripture and quote it to yourself as you begin to feel irritation beginning to build up. For example, **"Be quick to listen, slow to speak, and slow to anger, for the anger of man does not achieve the righteousness of God"** (James 1:19-20). Another example is thanking God for specific irritants since Scripture commands us to be **"thankful for all things for this is the will of God in Christ Jesus concerning you"** (1 Thessalonians 5:18). Often, simply saying to yourself **"love is patient"** helps tremendously when tension is mounting. Feeling impatient or frustrated are the emotions we experience as we think sinfully angry or selfish thoughts. We should confess this sin to God while it is at the mental attitude stage before it is outward sin.

2. "Love is kind."

Being kind is a key to creating the proper atmosphere in the home, church, or workplace. Kindness is shown in a gentle tone of voice and in kind acts. Kindness draws people to us whereas criticism and harshness pushes them away. This should not be a surprise as **"it is the kindness of God that leads us to repentance"** (Romans 2:4). We should think of ways to express kindness to others. For example, someone in your family becomes aggravated with a project they are trying to complete because the instructions are not clear. We could kindly say, "I'm sorry that this is so aggravating. Is there anything I can do to make it easier for you?" Speaking in a kind tone of voice and doing kind acts can be done by the grace of God.

3. "Love is not jealous."

Jealousy is fear of being displaced by another person or thing. It may be a valid concern or it may be a **"vain imagination"** (2 Corinthians 10:5,KJV). Either way, it is self-focused and self-concerned. Instead, we can show love by being glad for the other person that they have, for example, a new friend. Another example of showing love instead of jealousy is a wife being glad for her husband when he has the opportunity to visit with his family or play golf.

4. "Love does not brag."

Love does not boast. The Greek word for "brag" means to "talk conceitedly." Conceit is an "excessive appreciation of one's own worth."[47] Many times we boast about our relationships with others. We may take people for granted thinking that we deserve the nice things our family and friends do for us. Anyone can hold to an underlying belief that they deserve more. Instead, God wants our boasting to be done **"in the Lord"** (2 Corinthians 10:17). Then we will be gratefully giving God the credit instead of boasting from a proud heart about ourselves or our relationships with others.

5. "Love is not arrogant."

An arrogant heart is full of self-importance. You will find it difficult to tell an arrogant person anything. They are opinionated and defensive when disagreed with, reproved, or corrected. Arrogant and "know it all" is how we act when we are prideful. Anyone who is proud is likely to hurt others deeply. Instead of being arrogant, we should show love by being a humble servant to others, listen carefully to their opinions, and consider the possibility that we may be wrong or misinformed.

6. "Love does not act unbecomingly."

We act unbecomingly when we are rude or disrespectful to others. Often, we act unbecomingly based on our mood. Instead we should show love to all men by acting properly and in a manner that is pleasing to God.

7. "Love does not seek its own (way)..."

A lack of love is selfish. Selfishness is a common problem that pastors and counselors encounter. We should be more concerned with what we can do for others than what they can do for us. It would help greatly to show love instead of selfishness by thinking, "I need to consider that person to be more important than myself. What can I do to show love to them?" (see Philippians 2:4).

8. "Love is not provoked."

Showing love means that we control ourselves even under very difficult circumstances. The sad fact is that we are sometimes irritated and provoked even when the circumstances are not especially difficult. A Christian shows love by having the godly character quality of self-control. They realize that **"no temptation has overtaken you but such as is common to man; and God is faithful, who will not allow you to be pressured beyond what you are able, but with the pressure will provide the way of escape also, that you may be able to endure it"** (1 Corinthians 10:13). Instead of becoming provoked, we should show love by responding with patience and kindness.

9. "Love does not take into account a wrong suffered."

One way to show love is by not holding onto your bitterness, by forgiving, by not bringing up the past to others, and by not replaying bitter thoughts to ourselves in our mind. Catching yourself and correcting your thoughts are a tremendous way to show love. Rehearsing the offense suffered is unloving as it is "taking into account a wrong suffered."

10. "Love does not rejoice in unrighteousness but rejoices in the truth."

A loving person is one who not only deals properly with the sin in her life, but also does not entice, influence, or provoke others to sin. She tells others the truth. One of the by-products of being righteous is that they are, at the same time, showing love. Another way we can show love to others is by **"stimulating them to love and good deeds"** through encouraging them and supporting them to be godly and to do godly deeds (Hebrews 10:24).

11. "Love bears all things."

"Bearing all things" includes times when, for instance, a husband is being selfish or when he is having a tough time at work. His wife is committed to him, and he knows it. Loving involves sacrifice of self and it is important to remember that if she must suffer, it should be for **"doing what is right"** (1 Peter 3:17).

12. "Love believes all things."

Biblical love paints the other person in the best possible light. In other words, we are to show love to others by believing the best instead of assuming the worst about what they say or do or their motives. When at times, the "worst" is a fact, then we are to order our lives and our goals by faith and not by sight. So, no matter what others have done, godly, loving Christians trust in God's sovereign care. They know that God has a purpose in the circumstances for them. They believe, without a doubt, that He *can* **"work all things together for good to those that love Him"** (Romans 8:28).

13. "Love hopes all things."

Every Christian's hope is based on Jesus Christ and **"In Him [they] will not be disappointed"** (Romans 10:11, adaptation added). Their hope is a confident expectation, not just wishful thinking. Their hope is rooted in the Eternal King of Glory, the all-powerful Creator of the Universe who will eventually **"bring it to pass"** (1 Thessalonians 5:24). An outgrowth of her hope in God is hope that her loved ones will become more and more godly if they are Christians and perhaps be saved if they are not. "All things" (that love hopes) encompasses every aspect of their lives and their relationships with others. They should tell themselves things like, "She has disappointed me, but God never will. God can use what has happened to put pressure on her to repent."

14. "Love endures all things."

This Christian sees trials and pressures as coming into her life for a special opportunity to become more like the Lord Jesus. She does not usually enjoy those difficult times, but she does endure them with God's help. She shows love as Jesus did when He **"endured the cross, despising the shame"** (Hebrews 12:2). Why did He do it? **"...for the joy** that was set before Him" (Hebrews 12:2). Likewise, we can choose to show love to God and to others as we righteously endure trials and pressures in relationships with others. We can tell ourselves, "This is especially difficult, but with God's grace I can endure." And we can think, "Every day that I endure this I am showing love to God as 'love endures all things'."

Conclusion

The attitude of a Loving Heart is not last in this section because it is the least of the attitudes. It is last because it is the best. Basically we can think of a loving heart's attitude as manifested in two ways — love for God through obedience to Him and love for others through being patient, kind, etc. The ability to love God with every part of our being and to love others, including our enemies, is a grace of God and an evidence of our salvation. First, God loves us. Next, He saves us. Then, He produces the fruit of love in our lives.

The Pharisees had rules and they were self-righteous. The Lord Jesus wants us to obey God's Word because we love Him and want to please Him. He wants us to delight in the fact that He is working in our hearts to enable us to love others by following His example. We are to diligently "pursue love" and put God first. We are to "put on love" by thinking and responding in a practical, loving manner whether we feel like it or not. We Christians, of all people, should be known by our love.

❦

Chapter 13

Study Questions

1. What are the two greatest commandments in God's Law? Give the Scripture reference.

2. What does it mean to love God with all your heart, soul, and mind?

3. How do we show our love to God? What is to be our attitude? See 1 John 5:3.

4. According to 1 John 4:7,8,19, where does our ability to love one another come from? Why is it important?

5. What is the supreme example of how love acts? Give Scripture references.

6. According to 1 John 4:17-18, how is it that we can have confidence in the day of judgment?

7. What is wrong with this statement? - "God does not expect me to love my enemies."

8. What are we commanded to pursue in 1 Corinthians 14:1?

9. According to the first point under "Application of the Attitude of a Loving Heart" on page 210, what would be your desire if you love God? Ask yourself, "Does this describe me? Do I really love God?" If not, what is your prayer?

10. For each of the following manifestations of love, give one example from your own life in which you have been unloving and how, instead, you can be loving:
    a. Love is patient.

    b. Love is kind.

    c. Love is not jealous.

d. Love does not brag.

e. Love is not arrogant.

f. Love does not act unbecomingly.

g. Love does not seek its own (way).

h. Love is not provoked.

i. Love does not take into account a wrong suffered.

j. Love does not rejoice in unrighteousness but rejoices in the truth.

k. Love bears all things.

l.   Love believes all things.

m.   Love hopes all things.

n.   Love endures all things.

Final Conclusion

There is no such thing as "instant holiness" even though I felt holy right after the Lord saved me. The transforming of our minds from the world's way of thinking to God's perfect way is a process. It is a process that takes time, God-given diligence, and a focus on His worth, His glory, and His significance. My prayer for you is that God will use this book in your life to help you be more discerning about wrong thinking and sinful worldly heart's attitudes and that He will give you the heart of Daniel – a great reverence that causes you to bow before Him as *God Most High*.

> *And do not be conformed to this world, but be transformed by the renewing of your mind, so that you may prove what the will of God is, that which is good and acceptable and perfect.*
>
> **Romans 12:2**

Addendum

Salvation Work Sheets

By
Martha Peace

"Therefore having been justified by faith, we have peace with God through our Lord Jesus Christ, through whom also we have obtained our introduction by faith into this grace in which we stand; and we exult in hope of the glory of God."   **Romans 5:1-2**

Worksheet Number 1

"Who is Jesus Christ?"

The Bible tells us much about Jesus and who He is. Many of the claims were made by Jesus Himself and many were made by others about Him. Look up the following references and write down what these claims are. Before you begin your study, say a brief prayer to God and ask Him to show you if these things are true.

1. What does Jesus call himself?

   a. John 4:25,26

   b. John 8:28 and John 9:35-38

   c. Matthew 27:42,43

"Son of God" and "Son of Man" are Old Testament expressions for the Messiah who was predicted to come. The Prophets in the Old Testament knew that this Messiah was God and that He was worthy of worship. See Daniel 7: 13,14

2. What does Jesus claim about Himself?

   a. John 5:39

b. John 6:51

c. John 8:12

d. John 8:58

e. John 10:30 and 14:7-9

3. God the Father, God the Son, and God the Holy Spirit are all different manifestations of the one true God and they are all equal. However, when Jesus lived here on earth for 33 years, He subordinated himself to the will of God the Father. Why?
See Philippians 2:5-8

4. The Apostle Paul says in his letter to Titus that "God is our Savior" (Titus 1:3).

    a. Whom does Paul then say our Savior is? Titus 1:3,4

    b. What else does Paul say about Jesus? Colossians 1:15,16

5. Whom did Peter say that Jesus was?

   a. Mark 8:27-29

   b. 2 Peter 1:1

6. Whom did John the Baptist say that Jesus was?
John 1:29 and 34

7. Whom did the Apostle John say Jesus was?

   a. John 1:1,14

   b. Revelation 19:16

8. Whom did God the Father say Jesus was?
Matthew 3:17

9. Who has the authority to forgive sins?

   a. Luke 5:21

b. Who forgave the paralytic's sins? Luke 5:17-20

c. What did Jesus do to prove that He had authority to forgive sins? Luke 5:21-24

Summary:

Jesus claimed to be God by saying He:
>—was the "Son of God"
>—was the "Son of Man"
>—was the Savior (the Messiah)
>—had authority to forgive sins

Jesus proved that He was God by:
>—the works that He did (for example, creation)
>—the miracles that He did
>—His resurrection from the dead

The teaching of the Bible that Jesus is God is not something that we can explain by human logic. It is a supernatural truth which we believe because God's Spirit illumines the truth to us. In the next lesson, we will study in detail what Jesus did on the cross.

Worksheet Number 2

What Jesus Did on the Cross

Just about everyone in America has heard of Jesus and knows that He died on the cross. However, they may have many misconceptions about the purpose of His death. So, this week's lesson is a study on "What Jesus Did on the Cross."

1. How was Jesus killed? Matthew 27:35

2. What did the sign over His head say? Mark 15:26

3. What did the people say who were making fun of Jesus? Luke 23:35-37

4. How did the soldiers decide to divide up Jesus' garments? John 19:24

5. Which four books in the Bible contain the story of Jesus' death on the cross?

6. Make a list of what Jesus said as He was on the cross:
   a. Luke 23:34

   b. Luke 23:42,43

   c. Luke 23:46

   d. John 19:25,26

   e. John 19:30

   f. Mark 15:37,38

7. What was the purpose of Jesus' death?
   a. 1 Peter 2:24

b. Hebrews 2:17 ("propitiation" means to satisfy God's wrath)

c. Ephesians 1:7 ("In Him" refers back to Jesus Christ)

d. Romans 4:25 ("He" refers back to Jesus)

e. Romans 5:9

f. 1 Corinthians 15:3

Jesus told His disciples that the "Scriptures" (The Old Testament) were about Him. (John 5:39) Indeed, there are many places in the Old Testament that fore-tell of the coming Messiah and what He will do for the people so that they can be reconciled to God. (Sin had put a barrier between people and God because God is holy.) Jesus' death on the cross was God's way of punishing sin so that God's sense of justice could be satisfied. In other words, Jesus was punished in our place.

One of the most detailed descriptions of how Jesus took our punishment is in Isaiah 53. This was written by Isaiah over 700 years before Jesus was born. God gave this information to Isaiah supernaturally and Isaiah doesn't call Jesus by His name but calls him the "Servant".

8. How was Jesus treated by men? Isaiah 53:3

9. What did He "bear" for us? Isaiah 53:4

10. What happened to Jesus because of our "transgressions" (our sins) and our "iniquities" (also means sins)? Isaiah 53:5

11. Isaiah 53:5 says, "The chastening (punishment that we deserve) for our _____ fell upon Him."

12. Isaiah 53:6 says, "But the LORD has caused the iniquity (sin) of us all to _____ _____ _____"

13. What kind of sacrificial offering was Jesus? Isaiah 53:10

14. Where was Jesus' anguish? Isaiah 53:11

15. What will He bear? Isaiah 53:11

16. Isaiah 53:12, "Yet He Himself bore the _____".

17. What was God's motive for sending Jesus to die for our sins?
    1 John 4:10

Summary:

Jesus died on the cross to take the punishment for our sins. He
died in our place. He paid the full penalty and then He said,
"IT IS FINISHED!"

Worksheet Number 3

What Does the Bible Teach About Sin?

Last week we studied Jesus' death on the cross and we learned that He died to take the punishment for our sin. Also, we learned that God was satisfied that sin had been sufficiently punished and that Jesus' resurrection from the dead is proof of that. Today, we are going to study about sin — who sinned first, why they did, and why and how we sin today. Some sins are very obvious — for example, murder. Some sins are obvious only to God. Regardless of which kind of sin we commit, all sin grieves God because He is perfectly pure and holy. Therefore, we need to understand just what sin is and how to properly deal with it

1. The first created being to sin was an angel named Lucifer (later his name became Satan). His problem was pride. He wanted to be worshiped like God was worshiped by some of the other angels. Lucifer made a "power-play" in heaven and God cast Lucifer and all his followers out. What did Lucifer want? See Isaiah 14:13-14. List the five "I will" statements of Lucifer:

    a.

    b.

    c.

    d.

    e.

2. Lucifer had a real problem with pride. He should have been grateful to worship and serve God. Instead, he wanted all the attention himself. What was the underlying reason that he thought he deserved that kind of attention? Ezekiel 28:17

3. Lucifer was the first angel to sin and Adam and Eve were the first human beings to sin. When God created Adam and Eve they were innocent and without sin. God put them in the Garden of Eden which had a perfect environment and then God tested their devotion to Him and God told them they could eat fruit off any tree except one — "the tree of the knowledge of good and evil." God warned them that if they disobeyed, they would die.

   a. Satan was not content to leave well enough alone. He decided to try to get Adam and Eve to follow him by disobeying God. He appeared to Eve in the form of a serpent.
   See Genesis 3:1

   1) How is the serpent described?

   2) What did he ask Eve?

   b. God told Eve if she ate from that tree she would die. What did Satan tell her would happen? Genesis 3:4

c. Whom did Satan tell Eve she would be "like" if she ate? Genesis 3:5

d. What did Eve decide to do? Genesis 3:6

e. Before they sinned, Adam and Eve were very comfortable around God and not afraid of Him. What was their response to God now? Genesis 3:10

f. God confronted them with their sin. Whom did Adam blame? Genesis. 3:12

g. Whom did Eve blame? Genesis 3:13

4. Because God is holy, He has to punish sin. He pronounced judgment right then on Satan, Eve, and Adam. What was one part of the punishment? Genesis 3:19

5. After Adam and Eve sinned, they knew sin in a personal, experiential way. It had become part of their natural nature and was then passed down to their children and their children's children, etc. Also, the consequences of sin were passed down.

a. Why did "death spread to all men"? Romans 5:12

b. What is the "just" consequence of sin? Romans 6:23

6. The Bible classifies sin by different terms such as transgression, iniquity, wickedness, evil, disobedience, and unbelief. Look up the following verses and list what the particular sin is:
   a. Romans 13:1

   b. 1 Corinthians 6:18

   c. Ephesians 4:25-29 (these sins are obvious sins)

   d. Ephesians 4:31 (these sins may be obvious or may be "mental attitude" sins. Mental attitude sins are sins that we "think" which may or may not result in an additional obvious sin.)

   e. Ephesians 5:18

   f. Philippians 4:6

g. James 3:6

h. James 4:17

i. James 5:12

7. All sin, whether open or hidden, is seen and remembered by God. What does God judge? Hebrews 4:12

8. Is there anything hidden from God? Hebrews 4:13

9. God is holy. Therefore, He must punish sin. Man sins. Therefore, man is separated from God and the result is death. However, God loves man. So, He provided a way for man's sins to be punished and for man to be with Him for all eternity. The way that God provided is Jesus' death on the cross bearing our punishment. How is it that we can know that we, personally, are in a right relationship with God? That our sins are taken care of? See Acts 16:31

10. Oftentimes, people know about Jesus but they are still depending partly on themselves to be good enough to earn their way into heaven. If that's the case, then they are not really "believing" (trusting) in Jesus' death on the cross to be sufficient to save them. The Bible says that Jesus saves us **"not on the basis of deeds which we have done, but according to His mercy"** (Titus 3:5). In addition to not trusting the Lord Jesus as their Savior, many people are like Satan in that they do not want God to rule over them. They want to control their own lives, so they do not trust Christ as their Lord. If that is true of you, **"God is now declaring to men that all everywhere should repent, because He has fixed a day in which He will judge the world in righteousness through a Man [Jesus Christ] whom He has appointed, having furnished proof to all men by raising Him from the dead"** (Acts 17:30-31, adaptation added). Romans 10:9 tells us **"if you confess with your mouth Jesus as Lord, and believe in your heart that God raised Him from the dead, you shall be saved"**.

Worksheet Number 4

Assurance of Salvation

Many times when people are asked the question, "Do you know for sure that if you died you would go to heaven?" their answer is something like, "I'm not sure but I hope so." Today, our lesson will focus on what the Bible teaches about "knowing for sure." Because this issue is a critical one, before you begin to answer the questions, pray and ask God to show you the truth of His Word.

1. A person who is "saved" is going to heaven when he dies. What do you have to "do" to get "saved?"

    See John 3:16

    See Romans 10:13

    See John 1:12

2. Read the following verses and make a chart. On the left side, list what "saves" you and on the right side, list what will not "save" you:

    John 14:6

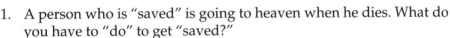

Ephesians 2:8,9

Acts 16:30,31

Ephesians 2:4,5

Colossians 1:13,14

Galatians 1:3,4

Titus 3:4-7

3. People think about their salvation one of two ways — they must be good and do things to "earn" it, or, Jesus did all the work necessary and they must put their faith or "trust" in Him (alone) to be their Savior.

   a. Nowhere does the Bible say that a person is saved by what he does or how good he is!!! On the contrary, the Bible says that the only acceptable sacrifice or punishment for sins is Jesus' sacrifice on the cross. Why, then, do so many people think they must believe in Jesus plus "earn" their way into heaven? Because, it is logical from a human perspective. But God says, "My ways are not your ways and my thoughts are higher than your thoughts." We're not holy so we do not think as God thinks. Because He's holy, all sin must be punished. It is not enough for us to have done more good things than bad. All the bad had to be dealt with and that's what Jesus declared when He said, "It is finished!"

b. Look up the following verses and write down what God wants you to know about assurance of your salvation.

1. Romans 3:28

2. Romans 8:1

3. Romans 10:11

4. John 5:24

5. John 6:47

6. 1 Corinthians 3:15

7. 2 Corinthians 1:9-10

8. 1 John 5:11-13

9. 1 Peter 1:3-5

10. Titus 1:2

4. There are basically three reasons why people don't have the assurance of their salvation:

a. They don't know what the Bible teaches, or they don't believe it.

b. They have never really put their trust in Jesus as their Lord and Savior. Jesus said, **"But you do not believe, because you are not of My sheep. My sheep hear My voice, and I know them, and they follow me; and I give eternal life to them, and they shall never perish and no one can snatch them out of My hand"**
(John 10:26-28).

c. There is no evidence of salvation in their life such as a desire for God, a longing to please God, or obedience to Christ's commandments. **"And by this we know that we have come to know Him, if we keep His commandments"** (1 John 2:3).

Salvation is a work of God not a work of man. So if you are having doubts, ask God to grant you repentance from your sin and faith in His Son.

"Put Off" – "Put On" Dynamic

This Bible study is for the purpose of teaching Christians how to deal practically with their sin. Many times we are aware that changes need to be made in our lives and we confess the appropriate sins to God. However, we may find ourselves committing those same sins again and again. Habitual sin is especially difficult because we automatically respond wrongly, without thinking. Therefore, it is important to learn exactly what God has to teach us through His Word about establishing new habit patterns.

Before you begin this study, pray and ask God to show you the truth of His Word.

Begin by looking up the following Scriptures and write out the answers to the questions.

1. How do we become aware of sin?
   a) Hebrews 4:12

   b) John 16:7-8

2. Do we have to sin? Explain. (See Romans 6:6,7,14.)

3. Describe what the "old self" was like. (See Ephesians 4:22.)

4. Describe what the "new self" is like. (See Ephesians 4:24.)

5. What are we to "put off" and what are we to "put on"?
   (See Ephesians 4:22,24.)

6. What are we to "put off" (lay aside) according to Colossians 3:9?

7. What are we to "put on" according to Colossians 3:10?

8. This "new self" is to be renewed. How? (See Colossians 3:10.)

Thus, we have seen that we are to "put off" our old ways of thinking and acting and "put on" new ways which are like those of Jesus Christ. When sinful ways of thinking or responding have become habitual, just confessing that sin is not enough. The sinful habit pattern must be replaced with a righteous habit pattern. It is as if what we are to "put on" is the biblical antidote to what we are to "put off". For example, it is not enough to just stop telling lies. A person must begin (work at) telling the truth, the whole truth. By God's help (grace) he will become a truthful person instead of a liar.

Look up the following Scriptures and fill in the chart:

Scripture Reference	"Put Off" Character Deficiencies	"Put On" Character Qualities
1. Ephesians 4:25		
2. Ephesians 4:26,27		
3. Ephesians 4:28		
4. Ephesians 4:29		
5. Ephesians 4:31,32		

6. Ephesians 5:11		
7. Ephesians 5:4		
8. Ephesians 5:18		
9. Philippians 4:6		
10. Colossians 3: 8,12,13,14		
11. Romans 13:12-14		

As we have seen earlier, God gives Christians the Holy Spirit to convict them of sin and to help them carry out God's desires. As a result, is there anything that God requires that a Christian cannot do? (See Philippians 4:13.) Hence, God will never ask us to do something that He will not give us the grace to carry out. Sometimes we may not feel like obeying God; however, if we do obey (in spite of our feeling), God will give us grace.

Write down the specific sins in your life you know need to be "put off".

Take time to confess these sins to God.

Write down what you are to "put on" (biblical antidote) in your life in the place of these sins:

Write down some practical actions you can do to "put on" godly character:

1.

2.

3.

4.

5.

Based upon what you have learned in this study, write out your prayer:

End Notes

[1] Tozer, A.W. *The Knowledge of the Holy* (San Francisco: Harper and Row, 1961), page 3.

[2] Tozer, page 28.

[3] Microsoft Encarta 98 Encyclopedia

[4] Encarta 98

[5] Encarta 98

[6] Encarta 98

[7] Nicholi, Armand M, Jr. *New Harvard Guide to Psychiatry* (Harvard, 1988), page 117-8.

[8] Nicholi, page 116.

[9] Freud, Sigmund. *New Introductory Lectures on Psychoanalysis* (New York:W.W. Norton & Company,Inc., 1933),p.45.

[10] Torrey, E. Fuller. *Freudian Fraud* (New York, New York: Harper Collins Publishers, 1992), pages 9-13.

[11] Vitz, Paul. *Sigmund Freud's Christian Unconscious* (Grand Rapids, Michigan: William B. Eerdmans Publishing Company, 1988), page 215.

[12] Edwards, Paul, Editor in Chief. *The Encyclopedia of Philosophy* (Macmillan Pub. Company, Inc. and The Free Press, 1967), page148.

[13] For more information regarding healing from past traumas I recommend Ed Bulkley's book, *Only God Can Heal the Wounded Heart* (Harvest House Publishers: Eugene, Oregon), 1995.

[14] Encarta 98.

[15] Nicholi, page 134.

[16] Nicholi, page 134, emphasis added.

[17] Piper, John. *The Pleasures of God* (Portland, Oregon: Multnomah,1991), page 39.

[18] Welch, Edward. *When People are Big and God is Small* (Phillipsburg, New Jersey: P&R Publishing, 1997), page 19.

[19] Erikson, Erik H. *Identity, Youth and Crisis* (New York: W.W. Norton & Company, Inc., 1958).

[20] Ibid, page 91-92.

[21] Ibid, page 93.

[22] Ibid, page 96-97.

[23] Nicholi, page 133.

[24] Encarta 98.

[25] Erikson, page 139.

[26] Nicholi, page 134.

[27] Meier, Paul; Minirth, Frank; Wichern, Frank. *Introduction to Psychology and Counseling Christians Perspectives and Applications* (Grand Rapids, Michigan: Baker Book House, 1982), page 16.

[28] Dr. Robert L. Thomas, "General Revelation and Biblical Hermeneutics" (The *Master's Seminary Journal*, Vol. IX, no.1).

[29] Tozer, page 27.

[30] Pink, Arthur, *The Attributes of God* (Grand Rapids, Michigan: Baker Publishing Company, 1975), page 41.

[31] Sproul, R.C., *The Holiness of God* (Wheaton, IL: Tyndate House, 1985).

[32] Tozer, page

[33] Watson, Thomas, *A Body of Divinity* (Carlisle, PA:Banner of Truth, reprint 1992).

[34] *The Hymnal for Worship & Celebration*, (Waco, Texas: Word Music, 1986), page 378.

[35] Adapted with permission from *Found: God's Will* by John MacArthur.

[36] Editors Merrill Tenney and Steven Barabas, *The Zondervan Pictorial Encyclopedia of the Bible* (Grand Rapids, Michigan: Zondervan Publishing House,1975), Volume Four, page 920.

[37] Adapted with permission from Stuart Scott's material "Decision Making God's Way," Biblical Counseling Advanced Course, Grace Community Church, Sun Valley, California.

[38] Fettke, Tom, Senior Editor, *The Hymnal for Worship and Celebration* (Waco, Texas: Word Music, 1986), page 479.

[39] MacArthur, John. *The MacArthur Study Bible* (Nashville, Tennessee: Word Publishing, 1997), page 1779, adapted from the footnote on chapter 10, verse 5.

[40] For more information on "Putting-Off and Putting-On" see the Bible study in the addendum of this book.

[41] *Webster's Seventh New Collegiate Dictionary* (Springfield, Massachusetts: G.&C. Merriam Company, 1963), page 57.

[42] Unknown author, *The Weed with an Ill Name* (Conrad, MT: Triangle Press, 1989).

[43] Scott, Stuart. *The Exemplary Husband* (Bemidji, MN: Focus Publishing, 2000), p.363.

[44] Ferguson, Sinclair B., *The Sermon on the Mount* (Edinburgh: the Banner of Truth Trust, 1987), p.104.

[45] MacArthur, John, *The MacArthur New Testament Commentary, Romans* (Chicago: Moody Bible Institute, 1994), p.249.

[46] Adapted from *The Excellent Wife* book by Martha Peace (Bemidji, MN:Focus Publishing,1995)p.100-102

[47] *Webster's Seventh New Collegiate Dictionary* (Springfield, Massachusetts: G.&C. Merriam Company, 1093), p.171.

Biographical Sketch of Martha Peace

Martha was born, raised, and educated in and around the Atlanta area. She graduated with honors from both the Grady Memorial Hospital School of Nursing 3 year diploma program and the Georgia State University 4 year degree program. She has thirteen years work experience as a Registered Nurse, specializing in pediatric burns, intensive care, and coronary care. She became a Christian in June, 1979. Two years later, Martha ended her nursing career and began focusing her attention on her family and a ladies' Bible study class. For five years she taught verse-by-verse book studies. Then she received training and certification from the National Association of Nouthetic Counselors. NANC was founded by Dr. Jay Adams for the purpose of training and certifying men and women as biblical counselors.

Martha is a gifted teacher and exhorter. She worked for eight years as a nouthetic (biblical) counselor at the Atlanta Biblical Counseling Center, in College Park, Georgia, where she counseled women, children, and teenagers. She instructed for 6 years at Carver Bible Institute and College in Atlanta where she taught women's classes including "The Excellent Wife," "Raising Kids Without Raising Cain," "Introduction to Biblical Counseling," "Advanced Biblical Counseling," "Personal Purity," and "The Book of Esther." In Addition to **The Excellent Wife**, Martha has written **Becoming a Titus 2 Woman**. Her books and tapes are available through Bible Data Services, 1119 Montclair Drive, Peachtree City, GA 30269, (770) 486-0011, or E-Mail: marthapeace@mindspring.com. You may also obtain information from Martha's website: marthapeace.com.

Martha is active with her family in Faith Bible Church in Peachtree City, Georgia, where she teaches teenagers and ladies' Bible study classes. In addition, she conducts seminars for ladies' groups on topics such as "Raising Kids Without Raising Cain," "The Excellent Wife," "Developing a Titus 2 Women's Ministry," "Having a High View of God," and "Personal Purity."

Martha has been married to her high school sweetheart, Sanford Peace, for thirty-five years. He is an air traffic controller with the FAA, but his real work is as an elder at Faith Bible Church. They have two children, Anna Maupin who is married and lives in Sharpsburg, Georgia, and David who is also married and is a Paramedic/Firefighter for Fayette County, Georgia. In addition to their children, they have seven grandchildren, Nathan, Tommy, twin girls – Kelsey and Jordan, Caleb, Cameron and baby Carter.